HEIDEGGER'S
CONTRIBUTIONS TO
PHILOSOPHY

Studies in Continental Thought

HEIDEGGER'S CONTRIBUTIONS TO PHILOSOPHY

An Introduction

DANIELA VALLEGA-NEU

INDIANA University Press

Bloomington & Indianapolis

Publication of this book is made possible in part with the assistance of a Challenge Grant from the National Endowment for the Humanities, a federal agency that supports research, education, and public programming in the humanities.

This book is a publication of

Indiana University Press
601 North Morton Street
Bloomington, IN 47404-3797 USA

http://iupress.indiana.edu

Telephone orders 800-842-6796
Fax orders   812-855-7931
Orders by e-mail iuporder@indiana.edu

The paper used in this publication meets the minimum requirements of American National Standard for Information Sciences—Permanence of Paper for Printed Library Materials, ANSI Z39.48-1984.

Manufactured in the United States of America

Library of Congress Cataloging-in-Publication Data

Vallega-Neu, Daniela, date
Heidegger's Contributions to philosophy : an introduction / Daniela Vallega-Neu.
   p.   cm. — (Studies in Continental thought)
Includes bibliographical references and index.
ISBN 0-253-34234-1 (cloth) — ISBN 0-253-21599-4 (paper)
1. Heidegger, Martin, 1889–1976. Beiträge zur Philosophie. 2. Philosophy. I. Title. II. Series.
B3279.H48 B454 2003
193—dc21
2002152287
1 2 3 4 5   08 07 06 05 04 03

For Linda

Contents

Contents

Acknowledgments

The project that led to this book arose during the meeting of the Collegium Phaenomenologicum in Citta' di Castello, Italy, in July 2000. I had been invited to give the first lecture course in a three-week program dedicated entirely to Heidegger's *Contributions to Philosophy (From Enowning)*. My task was to introduce Heidegger's *Contributions* in relation to *Being and Time*. The responses to my lectures convinced me that it would be useful to publish them, and I owe to John Sallis the idea to expand them into a small book that would introduce *Contributions*.

My work on *Contributions* began in 1989, when the book (*Beiträge zur Philosophie (Vom Ereignis)*) was published as volume 65 of Heidegger's Gesamtausgabe. At that time I was studying in Freiburg with Friedrich-Wilhelm von Herrmann, who immediately set out to teach the *Beiträge* in his seminars. I owe him a lot in my understanding of this difficult work. Since then, I also had many occasions to read and discuss *Contributions* with Susan Schoenbohm, whose careful reading of and commentary on the manuscript of the present book have been most helpful to me. I further thank Arnold Webb for his careful editorial work and Alejandro Vallega for his aid and support.

TRAVEDONA, JUNE 2002

Abbreviations

B   Martin Heidegger, *Contributions to Philosophy (From Enowning)*, trans. Parvis Emad and Kenneth Maly (Bloomington: Indiana University Press, 1999).

BaT   Martin Heidegger, *Being and Time*, trans. Joan Stambaugh (Albany: State University of New York Press, 1996).

BPP   Martin Heidegger, *The Basic Problems of Phenomenology*, trans. Albert Hofstaedter (Bloomington: Indiana University Press, 1988).

C   Martin Heidegger, *Beiträge zur Philosophie (vom Ereignis)*, ed. F.-W. von Herrmann (Gesamtausgabe, vol. 65, Frankfurt a. M.: Klostermann, 1989).

GA 5   Martin Heidegger, *Holzwege*, ed. F.-W. v. Herrmann (Frankfurt am Main: Klostermann, 1977).

GA 9   Martin Heidegger, *Wegmarken*, ed. F.-W. v. Herrmann (Frankfurt am Main: Klostermann, 1976).

GA 24   Martin Heidegger, *Die Grundprobleme der Phaenomenologie*, ed. F.-W. v. Herrmann (Frankfurt am Main: Klostermann, 1984), second edition.

GA 66   Martin Heidegger, *Besinnung* (Frankfurt am Main: Klostermann, 1997).

SuZ   Martin Heidegger, *Sein und Zeit* (Tübingen: Max Niemeyer Verlag, 1984).

HEIDEGGER'S
CONTRIBUTIONS TO
PHILOSOPHY

INTRODUCTION

Contributions to Philosophy (From Enowning)[1] may be considered Heidegger's second major work after *Being and Time*.[2] This book is composed of a "Preview," a final part called "Be-ing," and six joinings or fugues (*Fugen*), which structure the basic relations and intentions of Heidegger's being-historical thinking (*seynsgeschichtliches Denken*) after the mid 1930s, i.e., following the so-called "turning" (*Kehre*) of his thought. There are indications that the plan for this second major work arose as early as 1932, when Heidegger was working on his essay "On the Essence of Truth."[3] Heidegger wrote *Contributions*, more specifically the Preview and the six joinings, in 1936–1937, after his errancy into the National Socialist movement, after his first lectures on Hölderlin (1934–35), and after he started rethinking the beginnings of Western metaphysics in his lecture course, *Introduction to Metaphysics* (1935). The last part of *Contributions*, "Being," was written in 1938 and may be considered Heidegger's attempt to rethink what he had tried to elaborate in the previous sections.[4] Concurrent with Heidegger's work on *Contributions*, we find his first three lecture courses on Nietzsche, his work "The Origin of the Work of Art," and the lecture course *Basic Questions of Philosophy*.[5] These works indicate

1. Martin Heidegger, *Contributions to Philosophy (From Enowning)*, trans. Parvis Emad and Kenneth Maly (Bloomington: Indiana University Press, 1999). German edition: *Beiträge zur Philosophie (vom Ereignis)*, ed. F. W. von Herrmann, Gesamtausgabe, vol. 65 (Frankfurt a. M.: Klostermann, 1989).
2. Martin Heidegger, *Being and Time*, trans. Joan Stambaugh (Albany: State University of New York Press, 1996). German edition: *Sein und Zeit* (Tübingen: Max Niemeyer Verlag, 1984).
3. As von Herrmann writes: " . . . already since spring 1932 Heidegger had projected the basic traits of *Contributions*. The thought 'from enowning' does not first begin with the date at which Heidegger started writing *Contributions*. This is why Heidegger can begin his manuscript with the note: 'What was held back in prolonged hesitation is here held fast, hinting, as an indicative measure for a shaping'*" (*Wege ins Ereignis. Zu Heidegger's "Beiträge zur Philosophie"* [Frankfurt am Main: Klostermann, 1994], p. 1).
4. See Martin Heidegger, *Beiträge zur Philosophie*, editor's "Nachwort."
5. Martin Heidegger, *Grundfragen der Philosophie. Ausgewählte "Probleme" der "Logik,"*

the context in which the philosopher worked during these years: a re-thinking of the beginning of Western metaphysics, a rethinking, through his reading of Nietzsche, of its end, and the thought of a new beginning of Western thought, which arises from his encounter with the works of Hölderlin and which seeks its concrete possibilities in reflections on the essence of language and art.

Yet it would be misleading to understand *Contributions* as arising simply out of this context. One does more justice to this work by considering how Heidegger attempts in it to bring to language an abysmal source out of which arises an articulation of thought which he develops further and dif-ferently in his public lectures and lecture courses. In *Contributions*, Heidegger attempts to say something that, while it is always present, re-mains in the background, largely unsaid, both in his public writings and speeches of the time and in those later on. Should we understand this at-tempt in *Contributions* as a "secret" writing, the deciphering of which would allow us to unravel the mind of the famous philosopher? Not ex-actly. We might rather view *Contributions* as a site of explorations which are daring and utterly strange for their time. This is why Heidegger pre-fers to keep his struggles and discoveries protected or disguised until he finds a more suitable time for their public exposure.[6] Moreover, this work gives us no answers to Heidegger's question of all questions: the question of being. Rather, it opens the question further, in more exploratory, origi-nal ways. The discoveries that this book might reveal are neither supposi-tions nor conclusions which one could apply to the rest of Heidegger's thought. What is most revolutionary in this book, and what opens new possibilities for thinking, is rather its performative aspect, what happens as one follows the motions of thinking that are written into it.

Contributions calls for a rethinking and re-evaluation of all Heidegger's work. Heidegger's public lectures and lecture courses could be seen as bridges to the heart of the matter. Unlike *Contributions*, his public lec-

---

ed. F.-W. von Herrmann, GA 45 (Frankfurt a. M.: Klostermann, 1984). This lecture course from winter 1936–37 may be considered the public version of the first two joinings that structure *Contributions* and that are dedicated to a rethinking of Western metaphysics both in its beginning and in its closure.

6. Heidegger had planned to have *Contributions to Philosophy* published even later than 1989.

tures are written in a language that engages the listeners and readers of the time and attempts to translate as far as possible thoughts that withdraw as one attempts to translate them into a standard theoretical or everyday language. This withdrawal does not occur because these thoughts are "secret" or "mystical" but because they require a transformation of language that cannot be forced or explained, a transformation that exceeds the power of a human subject. This transformation of language implies a shift away from its propositional character (based on an interpretation of language as a system of signs signifying something, i.e., the "object" of thought) to its "poietic" character (in the sense of the Greek word *poiesis*, which means "bringing forth"). The language of *Contributions* is poietic in a twofold sense: it enables the e-vent of being to appear as it appears in thinking and—in turn—it enables language and thinking to appear as events of be-ing. What the language of *Contributions* says is found *in* the performative motion, that is, in the occurrence of thinking and language, and not in something that this occurrence would present objectively.

The shift away from propositional thought to the poietic, performative character of thinking is a particularly prominent aspect in contemporary French and American deconstructive thinking. However strongly Heidegger might have resisted many of these contemporary currents because, among other things, they lack a be-ing-historical (*seynsgeschichtlich*) dimension which is essential to Heidegger's thought (the necessity of the preparation of another beginning of Western history, a destiny revealed in the truth of being), Heidegger's attempt to overcome metaphysics (especially the metaphysics of subjectivity), his recognition of the finitude and groundlessness (in the metaphysical sense) of being, and his emphasis on the facticity of being in *Being and Time* have strongly influenced contemporary deconstructive movements. These topics are radicalized even further in *Contributions to Philosophy*.

In *Contributions*, Heidegger attempts to leave behind, along with metaphysics, any transcendental thinking, including that of *Being and Time*. With respect to *Being and Time*, the thinking of *Contributions* radicalizes the overcoming of a metaphysics of subjectivity by no longer taking human *Dasein* as a starting point in order to move to its groundedness in the temporality of being as such. Rather, it begins questioning

out of this temporality of being itself (i.e., the truth of be-ing). The
question here is not one of how to break through or to open up subjectivity; it is rather — if we want to focus on human being — how human being
comes to be, how it finds an articulation in the openness and groundlessness of the event of being. *Contributions* also radicalizes the facticity of
Dasein by thinking (in) the overcoming of the ontological difference,
i.e., by thinking in the "simultaneity" (*Gleichzeitigkeit*) of being and beings without thereby re-instating a primacy of beings or slipping back
into a representational mode of thinking.

Other issues of wider contemporary interest prominent in *Contributions* are the questions of technology and power that Heidegger considers
under the notion of machination (*Machenschaft*), the possibility of rethinking the history of philosophy as events and articulations of being
(implying a departure from a historiographic and objective understanding of historical events and the possibility of rereading metaphysics non-
metaphysically), and a rethinking of the dimension of the godly (*das Gotthafte*) not as something above being but as an occurrence *of* being.

The peculiar character of *Contributions* makes access to this book particularly difficult. It was written without any didactical considerations; it appears fragmentary, repetitive, a collection of personal notes, incomplete
sentences, lists of words or topics, as well as longer, more elaborates passages. Heidegger's *Contributions to Philosophy* is more a site of struggle than
a systematic book that presents a step-by-step development of thoughts.
This does not mean that it is without rigor or shape. But the shape arises in
and as a struggle of rigorous thinking in which one can perceive an attempt
to give shape to emerging thoughts, thoughts that, at their inceptual stage,
echo their ungraspable source. At the same time, Heidegger's thinking in
Contributions encounters already embodied conceptualities and structures
that have arisen in two millennia of the history of Western philosophy and
that both facilitate and limit what he attempts to say.

This introduction to Heidegger's *Contributions* is written to facilitate
an approach to this difficult work for readers who already have some familiarity with other works of Heidegger (especially *Being and Time*). It is
written much more systematically than *Contributions* and attempts to
provide some directions and structure to help the reader orient herself in

this work. Yet, given the character of *Contributions*, what this introduction can offer are merely indications, directions; it is up to each reader to find her own encounter with Heidegger's work and to merge into the tonalities and movements of his thoughts. Much like in a dance lesson, one can learn the steps, but to repeat the steps does not yet mean that one is dancing. In reading *Contributions*, as in dancing, one can, perhaps, at best forget the steps and something different can come to be.

Given the prominent role that *Being and Time* has had in the past decades of Heidegger interpretation, this book will introduce Heidegger's *Contributions* first by rethinking *Being and Time* in the light of the transformative turn[7] that marks the passage between the two major works. It will, then, take up again basic issues of *Being and Time* within the context of *Contributions*' be-ing-historical thinking. The chapters thereafter will lead through each of the joinings that mark the composition of *Contributions*, ending with a crucial section (section 267 of *Contributions*) titled "Be-ing" from the final part of the book. Like each of the joinings, this last section attempts to articulate the whole domain of the truth of be-ing as *Ereignis*. But this time, enowning is not thematized by emphasizing one specific aspect or domain of its occurrence; instead, section 267 gathers all the different aspects that were previously discussed.

The particularity of the language of *Contributions* requires some remarks concerning translation. An adequate translation of Heidegger's *Beiträge zur Philosophie* is not possible. This is not only because every translation has to cope with a loss or shift of meaning in the transition from one language to another, but also because the transformation of thought in which Heidegger engages necessarily abandons the common use of language and, much like poetry, ventures into new possibilities of language. The possibility of playing with new combinations of prefixes and suffixes, of transforming verbs into nouns and vice versa, which the German allows, is not possible in the same way in English. Consequently, disagreements as to how certain words and passages of *Contributions*

7. I speak of a "transformative turn" and not of a "turning" in order to distinguish this turn from the turning (*Kehre*) which names, for Heidegger, the internal dynamics of the event of be-ing thought as enowning.

should be translated are inevitable. This book for the most part follows
the only available English translation by Parvis Emad and Kenneth
Maly. I have chosen different translations only where it appears important to me. Different translations are marked with an asterisk (*). An asterisk close to a word within a quotation mark indicates a different word
choice; an asterisk after the closing quotation mark indicates a difference
in phrasing or syntax. Each quotation will be followed first by the page
number of the English translation, with "C" for *Contributions*, and then
by the page number of the German book, with "B" for *Beiträge* (for ex-
ample: ". . . ." C75, B107). As far as *Being and Time* is concerned, quota-
tions will be drawn from the Joan Stambaugh translation and followed by
references to the German Max Niemeyer edition.

PART ONE

From *Being and Time* to *Contributions*

The following chapters propose first a reading of *Being and Time* in view of *Contributions* and then a reading of *Contributions* with reference to the earlier work. This will reveal both continuity in and major differences between Heidegger's earlier thought of "fundamental ontology" and the "be-ing-historical thinking" of *Contributions*. A reading of *Being and Time* in view of the later work *Contributions* is necessarily retrospective. Thematizing *Being and Time* in the context of *Contributions* already moves the earlier work into an encounter with the later, already (dis)places the question of the first work into the context of the other. Our focus thereby is directed to what gives itself to be thought in this (dis)placing encounter. What guides this reading of *Being and Time* is the transformative turn that marks the passage between the earlier and the later work, a transformative turn which implies a shift in the direction of thought and, more specifically, a shift in the way in which thinking finds its guidance and language. We will see that, whereas in *Being and Time* Heidegger exposes the question of being in a way that leads *toward* the origin (the temporal occurrence of being, which in *Contributions* he will reconsider as the truth of being), in *Contributions* Heidegger attempts to think *from* the origin (the truth of being as enowning). Among Heidegger scholars, this shift in the directionality of thought has been thematized and much discussed as the "turning" (*Kehre*) of Heidegger's thought in the thirties, a turning that he understands as originating in a more originary turning, namely, the turning that occurs in the event of the truth of be-ing (*Wahrheit des Seyns*)[1] as "enowning" (*Ereignis*).[2]

---

1. For Heidegger, the use of the word "*Seyn*" (instead of "*Sein*") indicates that being is not thought of metaphysically, i.e., it is not thought of analogously to beings as a (highest) being but rather as an occurrence (C307; B436). In order to render the non-representational and temporal character of being, "*Seyn*" is translated as "be-ing."
2. In this context, see Kenneth Maly, "Turnings in Essential Swaying and the Leap," in

Three thematic fields play a major role in the transformative turn of Heidegger's thinking at the beginning of the thirties. The first is what, in the "Letter on Humanism," he calls a failure (*Versagen*) to articulate the question of *Being and Time* in the language of metaphysics. This refers to a limit of the language, conceptuality, and the specific systematic approach of the earlier work. We will see that Heidegger's transcendental approach to the question of being, which finds its articulation in the notions of "transcendence," "horizon," and "condition of the possibility," is not able to adequately say what it attempts to say.

The second thematic field, as Heidegger states in section 262 of *Contributions* (C317; B451) and in *Besinnung*,[3] concerns the necessity of a more originary insertion of thinking into being's historicality (*Geschichtlichkeit*).[4] This includes not only a re-engagement with the history of Western philosophy (with particular emphasis on its beginning and closure), but also a deeper understanding of Heidegger's own thinking as historical (*geschichtlich*), i.e., as partaking in the historical event of be-ing.

The third thematic field arises out of Heidegger's engagement with Hölderlin and out of Heidegger's struggle with the Christian tradition, and concerns the rethinking of godliness within the question of being. In *Contributions*, the "godly" is considered as an essential constituent of being's occurrence. This, by the way, does not mean that Heidegger's philosophy becomes a theology. Heidegger continues to stress the primacy of the question of be-ing *within* which the dimension of the godly appears. More specifically, the godly arises in the necessity to ground be-ing in beings, to prepare a historical site in which be-ing may occur inceptively.

Companion to Heidegger's "Contributions to Philosophy," ed. Charles E. Scott, Susan M. Schoenbohm, Daniela Vallega-Neu, and Alejandro Vallega (Bloomington and Indianapolis: Indiana University Press, 2001), pp. 150–170.
3. Martin Heidegger, "Mein bisheriger Weg," in *Besinnung*, Gesamtausgabe, vol. 66 (Frankfurt a. M.: Klostermann, 1997), p. 415 (in the following quoted as GA 66, 415). This book was written shortly after *Contributions*.
4. Heidegger differentiates "*Geschichte*" from "*Historie*," both of which are translated as "history" in English. Where "*Historie*" refers to past events from an objective, i.e., representational, point of view, "*Geschichte*" bears the sense of both "history" and "occurrence," thus marking the temporality as well as the epochality of being as it is disclosed in Da-sein, in being-t/here. For the difference between "*Geschichte*" and "*Historie*" see also Alejandro Vallega, "'Beyng-Historical Thinking,' in Heidegger's *Contributions to Philosophy*" (in *Companion to Heidegger's "Contributions to Philosophy"*), especially pp. 52–54.

1. A FAILURE OF LANGUAGE

In the "Letter on Humanism," Heidegger explains that the main problem that led him to interrupt the itinerary of *Being and Time* and seek a new way of posing the question of being was a failure (*Versagen*) of language. The problem was that *Being and Time* still attempted to use "the language of metaphysics."[1] At the same time, Heidegger maintains that already in this earlier work he questions being in a more original way than metaphysics. We may say, then, that in *Being and Time* Heidegger fails to say what he attempts to say. In *Besinnung,* Heidegger also explicitly notes that in *Being and Time* there is at work the attempt to be guided once again by "the basic ways of questioning" (*Grundfragestellungen*) of the history of metaphysics, but in a new beginning and point of view (GA 66, 413). Heidegger's approach remains indebted to metaphysics, especially in his "transcendental" approach to the question of being, which includes the notions of "*transcendence*," of "*horizon*," of "*condition of possibility*," and his thinking in terms of the *ontological difference*. But while, in *Being and Time*, Heidegger takes up anew the basic questionings of the history of philosophy, he does this by rethinking these questions so radically that he deconstructs the metaphysical tradition from which they arise and uncovers an utterly finite, non-metaphysical "abysmal ground"[2] of being,

---

1. In Martin Heidegger, *Basic Writings*, trans. David Farrell Krell (San Francisco: Harper San Francisco, 1992), p. 231. Martin Heidegger, "Brief über den Humanismus," in Gesamtausgabe, vol. 9 (Klostermann: Frankfurt a.M., 1976), p. 328. In the following referred to as (GA 9, 328).
2. "Abysmal" is the translation of the German "*abgründig,*" which usually indicates an unfathomable depth. The German word has less negative connotations than the English and is used by Heidegger to indicate a mode of disclosure which cannot be grasped in terms of presence and which withdraws from any kind of representation.

namely the temporal horizon in which being discloses and things come to presence. This temporal horizon, which in *Contributions* is reconceived as the *truth of be-ing*, is not a metaphysical ground in that it is not presented, analogously to beings, as a being of any kind, and in that it discloses finitely in Dasein's resolute being-towards-death. In this respect, Heidegger's first major work already pursues its questioning in a more originary way than the metaphysical tradition out of which it arises.

So—viewed retrospectively—*Being and Time* remains somewhat ambiguous, a work of transition, as Heidegger repeatedly points out in *Contributions*. Since this ambiguity is nothing one could overcome, the following reading of *Being and Time* involves a double task: that of showing how Heidegger uses the notions of transcendence, horizon, and the condition of possibility in a way that is radically different from metaphysics, and also that of showing that these notions and Heidegger's specific systematic approach inevitably point back toward metaphysics. In order to pursue this task we need to take a careful look at the directions of thought *Being and Time* takes, i.e., at *the movements of thought in the path of questioning*, which find their articulation in the notions of "transcendence," "horizon," and the "condition of possibility." We will see in the next chapter that one of the main differences between *Contributions* and *Being and Time* concerns precisely the directionality and the movements of thought and the way in which they come to language. The path of questioning (and accordingly the language) of *Being and Time* is imbedded in the project of fundamental ontology as a whole. This is why we need to reconsider the main task of *Being and Time* and the way Heidegger pursues it.

a) The Itinerary of Being and Time

Heidegger states that the first task of *Being and Time* is to explicate time as the transcendental horizon for the question of being.[3] This is

---

3. The title of Part One reads: "The interpretation of Dasein on the basis of temporality." The second part, the one that should have appeared as the third division of Part One under the title "Time and Being," was withheld, and, as Heidegger tells in *Besinnung* (GA 66, p. 413f), destroyed. A second attempt to work out this third division occurred in the lecture of SS 1927, *The Basic Problems of Phenomenology*.

what fundamental ontology is meant to prepare by way of an analysis of Dasein (of human being). An analysis of Dasein provides access to the question of being as such because Dasein has both "ontic" and "ontological" characteristics. Dasein is both an entity (a being) and, in its understanding of being, discloses being as such. As Heidegger states in section 4 of *Being and Time*, "The ontic distinction of Dasein lies in the fact that it *is* ontological" (BaT10; SuZ12), which means that Dasein is a being which, in distinction to other beings, is constituted in such a way that in its existence being as such is disclosed.[4] Thus, an analysis of Dasein intrinsically leads to the question of being as such.

Dasein understands itself pre-theoretically in its being, and thereby not only discloses possibilities of its own being but also of the being of beings in general (BaT11; SuZ13). As Heidegger emphasizes, this understanding of being (*Seinsverständnis*) is not a property of a being we call man, but it is rather "we that are always already involved in an understanding of being" (BaT4; SuZ5). It is out of this usually unquestioned, pre-theoretical understanding of being that we first come to know ourselves as well as other beings. The understanding of being that belongs to Dasein discloses at the same time Dasein's own possibilities of being, world, and beings that become accessible within the world (BaT11; SuZ13). It should be clear, then, that Heidegger does not take Dasein to be a self-enclosed subject that leads to the question of something other than itself (being as such). Rather, Heidegger questions being as such by way of an analysis of Dasein because Dasein, human *being*, is constituted as being in-the-world, which means that in Dasein a world and, thus, the being of beings in general is disclosed. Dasein is both a being (in an ontic sense) and is ontological (because it is open to being as such), and thus can serve as the being that is interrogated (*das Befragte*) in order to gain access to what is asked about (*das Erfragte*), namely, being as such.

In its pre-theoretical understanding of being, Dasein "stands out" (ek-

---

4. I suppose that the reader is familiar with the ontological difference between being (*Sein*) and beings (*Seiendes*), which is operative in the distinction between ontic and ontological. See also Martin Heidegger, *The Basic Problems of Phenomenology* (BPP), trans. Albert Hofstaedter (Bloomington: Indiana University Press, 1988), p. 227ff. German edition: *Die Grundprobleme der Phaenomenologie* (GA 24), ed. F.-W. v. Herrmann (Frankfurt am Main: Klostermann, 1984²).

sists) in the open horizon of being, and this is what in his essay "On the Essence of Ground"[5] Heidegger will call more explicitly the *"transcendental constitution"* of Dasein. Here, "transcendental" means that, in existing, Dasein occurs temporally as a transcending beyond beings into the disclosure of being as such, so that in this transcending not only its own possibilities of being but also the being of other beings is disclosed. We see here the ambiguity of Dasein: on the one hand, at the beginning of *Being and Time*, it is taken as a being that is questioned; on the other hand, in its existence (in its being), Dasein is always already beyond itself (transcends itself in terms of a being) in the temporal horizon of being as such and comes to be who it is out of this horizon. *In the itinerary of* Being and Time *Heidegger moves from this transcendental constitution of Dasein to the temporality as the meaning of Dasein's being, and then to the horizonal temporality as the meaning of being as such.* We will follow this itinerary more closely, starting with the transcendental constitution of Dasein.

Heidegger develops the transcendental constitution of Dasein's being as the unity of Dasein's three "existentials," i.e., of three aspects that structure Dasein's existence: projection (*Entwurf*), thrownness (*Geworfenheit*), and being with beings (*sein bei . . .*). In section 41 of *Being and Time* he says that Dasein is always already *ahead* of itself in its being. "Dasein* is always already 'beyond itself,' [. . .] as being toward the potentiality-for-being which it itself is" (BaT179; SuZ191f). Dasein does not first reach being by transcending itself as a being but occurs always already in being-ahead-of-itself. This "being-ahead-of-itself" occurs in Dasein's *projection.* Yet, being ahead of itself, that is, projecting itself into possibilities of being, Dasein is also always already *thrown* into a world and, thus, into possibilities of being that are consigned to it. Finally, in "being-ahead-of-itself-in-already-being-in-a-world," Dasein *is* also always already *with* inner-worldly things at hand. Projection, thrownness, and being with beings are the three existentials that constitute *care,* the being of Dasein. Heidegger finds this existential constitution of Dasein by inquiring into and analyzing Dasein in its everyday being in the world.

5. Martin Heidegger, "On the Essence of Ground," in *Pathmarks,* ed. William McNeill (New York: Cambridge University Press, 1998). German edition: "Vom Wesen des Grundes," in *Wegmarken* (GA 9), ed. F.-W. v. Herrmann (Frankfurt am Main: Klostermann, 1976).

The existential constitution of Dasein (care) must then be shown to be rooted in temporality, which step, in turn, leads to the disclosure of being as such out of being's temporality.

Before explicating care in terms of temporality, Heidegger explores the possible being-a-whole of Dasein in its being-towards-death. By questioning the possible being-a-whole of Dasein, Heidegger exposes the limits of its being-ahead-of-itself in already being-in-a-world, that is, the finitude of Dasein's transcending projection. This limit is not disclosed in our everyday being with inner-worldly things at hand, but is only disclosed when our everyday engagement with beings is interrupted or withdraws, as happens in the fundamental attunement of anxiety.[6] In anxiety, death is disclosed as the utmost possibility of Dasein, the possibility of being which is the possibility of not being at all. However, death is not simply a limit in a negative sense. Rather, Heidegger thinks of death as a limit in the same way that he reads the Greek word for limit: *peras*, that is, as a limit that gives something free in its limiting. Death is a limit that frees Dasein's ownmost potentiality of being (*eigenstes Seinkönnen*)[7] (BaT232; SuZ250). By comporting oneself toward death (not by attempting to flee it, but by being open to its possibility, i.e., by anticipating the possibility of not being), the possibility of being and not being first genuinely discloses. By anticipating its own death, the limit of its being, Dasein exists authentically.

In existing authentically, the finite whole of Dasein's possibility of being is disclosed, and this "whole" includes the being of other beings (BaT243f; SuZ264). In anticipation of death, then, being as such is disclosed out of the limit of Dasein's possibility of being. However, as Heidegger says at the end of section 53 of *Being and Time*, in the anticipatory being-towards-death we have only found the *ontological possibility* of being-a-whole. This ontological possibility *needs an ontic existentiell*[8] attestation (*Bezeugung*),

6. Heidegger calls anxiety a "fundamental attunement" (*Grundstimmung*) because it is not directed at any specific thing, but rather discloses being as such.
7. "*Eigenstes*" means "what is most peculiar to," "what is most 'own' to" in the sense of "what belongs most to."
8. In *Being and Time* "existential" and "existentiell" are distinguished precisely in that "existential" refers to the ontological structures that constitute Dasein's possibility of being, whereas "existentiell" refers to concrete possibilities of being that are taken over by Dasein.

which means that it needs to be found in a concrete mode of being. Why that? We may answer this question with what Heidegger says in the introduction to *Being and Time*, namely, "the roots of the existential analysis [. . .] are ultimately *existentiell*—they are *ontic*" (BaT11; SuZ13). This means that the ontological structure of Dasein (the existentiality of existence) must be disclosed in an existentiell way (factually); otherwise it could not become a phenomenon for philosophical inquiry. But, in turn, the condition of possibility of this existentiell, factual, disclosure of Dasein's most extreme possibility of being presupposes the disclosure of being itself. To put it briefly: The ontological is disclosed in the ontic, at the same time that the ontic presupposes the ontological as its "condition of possibility." Yet, in the itinerary of *Being and Time* Heidegger exposes the ontological structure of Dasein independently from its ontic existentiell opening.[9]

Heidegger finds the ontic attestation for Dasein's ontological possibility of being-a-whole in the "call of conscience." In his analysis of conscience in chapter two of the second division of *Being and Time*, Heidegger explores "anticipatory resoluteness" as Dasein's authentic mode of disclosure in which it explicitly chooses its authentic being-itself and its authentic possibility of being in being-towards-death. In this authentic possibility of being, Heidegger says, Dasein takes over "the fact that it *is* the not-ground* of its nothingness*" ("*der nichtige Grund seiner Nichtigkeit*")[10] (BaT283; SuZ306). The ground of Dasein's transcendence, which it reaches in thrown projection and takes over in anticipatory resoluteness, is permeated by "nothingness." This is the point where Heidegger's notion of transcendence discloses a "ground" of being that is utterly different from a metaphysical ground in that it has neither the character of presence nor of permanence, but is both finite and a temporal occurrence.

9. We will see this separation of "ontological structure" and "ontic attestation" disappear in *Contributions* where, one could say, the ontological is brought to thought and language in the moment of its ontic attestation. In other words, being is brought to language as it arises factually in thinking.

10. "*Nichtig*" is an adjective formed from the adverb "*nicht*" ("not"). A "*nichtiger Grund*" is a ground that has the "quality" of not occurring as a ground in the metaphysical sense. "*Nichtigkeit*" is a substantive formed from the adjective "*nichtig*" (related to "*nicht*") which in the figurative sense means "empty" or "void." As Heidegger uses it, it does not have a pejorative connotation. This is why I prefer a more literal translation of it as "nothingness" instead of using "nullity," as in the Stambaugh translation.

We should take a closer look at the way in which Heidegger arrives at this notion of a "not-ground" (*nichtiger Grund*), of a ground of being permeated by nothingness. In order to disclose Dasein's ownmost, finite possibility of being, Dasein's everyday involvement with beings needs to be interrupted. This occurs through the call of conscience, a call that occurs without sound (BaT252; SuZ273). "The call of conscience," says Heidegger, "has the character of *summoning* Da-sein to its ownmost potentiality-of-being-a-self, by summoning it to its ownmost quality of being a lack" (BaT249; SuZ269). Of course, here Heidegger is considering the call of conscience as an ontological term rather than as a psychological phenomenon. He emphasizes the disclosive function of conscience: "Conscience gives us 'something' to understand, it *discloses*" (ibid.). "What" consciousness discloses is Dasein's finitude (its being a "lack") and, with it, Dasein's ownmost possibility of being.

The disclosive power of the call of conscience requires a listening and responding to this call, which Heidegger calls "wanting-to-have-a-conscience." Wanting-to-have-a-conscience is the existentiell phenomenon that Heidegger sought when he looked for an ontic-existentiell attestation for Dasein's ontological possibility of being a whole. In wanting-to-have-a-conscience, Dasein chooses in an authentic existentiell way its ownmost possibility of being. As noted earlier, Heidegger calls this choice "resoluteness." Of course, we should keep in mind that this "choice" is not a choice made by a human subject. Rather, it is an occurrence that determines Dasein, involving a free response to the call of conscience, and, thus, a taking up of a disclosive mode of being.

With respect to the call of conscience, Heidegger distinguishes three aspects: the one summoned in the call, what is called, and the caller. That to which the call is addressed is Dasein as the everyday "they-self" (*Man selbst*), i.e., who Dasein is indistinctly in everydayness. The call interrupts Dasein's listening to the "they." In other words, the call interrupts a mode of being in which one does what "one" does without awareness of the meaning of one's own being. In the disclosiveness of the call "lies the factor of a jolt, of an abrupt arousal" (BaT251; SuZ271), says Heidegger; secondly, he says: "The call calls from afar to afar. It reaches him who wants to be brought back," back, of course, to his authentic, finite, and unique self. Thus, the call calls Dasein from its immersion in the they-self back to its own proper self (*das eigene Selbst*), that is, to its ownmost possibilities of being.

Thirdly, the "caller" in the call of conscience remains, as Heidegger says, in a "striking indefiniteness," which is a positive characteristic in the sense that "who" calls is nothing else but the calling. " *'Es' ruft,*" says Heidegger, "a calling occurs" that comes "*from* me, and yet *over* me" (BaT254; SuZ275). The caller is not determined by anything. It is "Dasein in its uncanniness, primordially thrown being-in-the-world, as not-at-home, the naked 'that' in the nothingness of the world" (BaT255; SuZ276). The caller is Dasein in its most primordial, finite thrownness, i.e., Dasein in its utmost possibility of being: the possibility of not being at all, which discloses the mere "that" of Dasein's existence.

The call of conscience turns out to be the call of care: "the caller is Dasein*, anxious in thrownness (in its already-being-in . . .) about its possibility-of-being. The one summoned is also Dasein, called forth to its ownmost possibility-of-being (its being-ahead-of-itself . . .). And what is called forth by the summons is Dasein*, out of falling prey to the they (already-being-together-with-the-world-taken-care-of . . .)" (BaT256; SuZ277). Thus the "toward what" (Dasein) and the "whence" (Dasein) of the call of conscience are the same occurrence. The call is "a calling back that calls forth (*ein vorrufender Rückruf*)" (BaT259; SuZ280).

After having thus related conscience back to the ontological structure of Dasein, Heidegger goes on to analyze what the call announces: guilt. This will lead us to the question of the "ground" of Dasein, the ground toward which and out of which Dasein always already transcends, a ground that, as we will see, is a temporal occurrence in which being as such is disclosed finitely.

Heidegger points to two formal characteristics of guilt (taken as an ontological notion): firstly, its "not" character, which refers to the fact that, in guilt, there is always a lack; secondly the character of "being-the-ground for" something (BaT261; SuZ283).[11] Thus Heidegger defines the

---

11. The German word for "guilt," "*Schuld,*" may be used in the sense of "owing something to someone," for instance money.

"formal existential idea of 'guilty' as being-the-ground for a being which is determined by a not—that is, *being-the-ground of a nothingness**" (*Grundsein einer Nichtigkeit;* ibid.). In this sense, guilt is a constitutive way of the being of Dasein. The "not" and the "being-the-ground of a nothingness" are constitutive of the being of Dasein, of care. They permeate all of Dasein's existentials, both in relation to determinate possibilities of being and in relation to the not-being that is disclosed in being-towards-death.

In relation to determinate possibilities of being, the "not" that permeates care is found in the fact that Dasein has to take over the possibilities and impossibilities (i.e., the "ground") into which it finds itself thrown and that, thus, Dasein never has power over this ground. In other words, Dasein does not make its possibilities of being but is thrown into them. So, one sense of the "nothingness" that Dasein *is* is its "powerlessness" over possibilities of being, a powerlessness that is consigned to Dasein and that it has to be in its being a ground. A second way in which Dasein is the ground of its nothingness is found in the fact that, in its thrownness, Dasein always stands in specific possibilities and, therefore, it always stands in possibilities which thereby remain excluded; it stands in the not of possibilities (BaT262f; SuZ284f). Dasein has to sustain (be the ground of) the fact that, in having to take over determinate possibilities of being into which it finds itself thrown, it cannot take over other concrete possibilities of being.

The third way in which Dasein is the ground of its nothingness concerns its relation to being-towards-death. Heidegger unfolds this in section 62 of *Being and Time.* In order to experience, in resoluteness, that being guilty, i.e., that being a not-ground of itself (a ground permeated by nothingness) always belongs to Dasein, Dasein's possibility of being must be disclosed to its end. This is how Heidegger relates resoluteness to Dasein's being-towards-death, that is, to the limit from which Dasein is disclosed as a whole. Being-towards-death is not a modality of being in addition to resoluteness, but is intrinsically the way in which resoluteness occurs. Resoluteness *"harbors in itself authentic being-towards-death as the possible existentiell modality of its own authenticity"* (BaT282; SuZ305). Conceived existentially, death is the possibility of there being no possibility of existence. Viewed in relation to Dasein's disclosiveness, death is the possibility of ultimate closure. Death is, as Heidegger says, the "absolute nothingness of Dasein" (BaT283; SuZ306).

We may now understand in a more complete sense Heidegger's sentence, "Resolutely, Dasein takes over authentically in its existence the fact that it *is* the not-ground of its nothingness" (ibid.). The not-ground has been explicated as the thrown ground (the disclosure of possibilities and impossibilities of being) that is "not" insofar as Dasein has no power over it and insofar as projecting oneself into some possibilities of being, other possibilities of being *are* not. With death in mind as the most extreme possibility of being, we see how Dasein's thrownness is also and more originarily a thrownness into its possibility of not being at all, and that the projection of Dasein is not only a projection toward determinate possibilities of being but also, at its originary limit, a projection toward its most extreme possibility of not-being.[12]

But, explicating the original being a not-ground (*nichtiger Grund*) into which Dasein is thrown and which it takes over in projection—both in relation to determinate possibilities of being and to the possibility of not being at all—does not yet reach the full meaning of this not-ground. Its full meaning appears only if we consider temporality. Without considering temporality, the not-ground of Dasein might be understood simply as a negation of being. But it is decisive to understand this not-ground as a temporal event which eventually will be unfolded as the meaning of being. By moving, with Heidegger, into his discussion of temporality (*Zeitlichkeit*) we also take with him the next step in the itinerary of *Being and Time*, a step which leads from the explication of Dasein's transcendental constitution to temporality as the meaning of Dasein's being, to the horizonal temporality (*Temporalität*) as the meaning of being as such.

Heidegger develops "temporality as the ontological meaning of care" in section 65 of *Being and Time*. The temporal meaning (*Sinn*) of care is

---

12. We find traced, here, the double sense of un-truth that Heidegger develops later in his essay, "On the Essence of Truth," which, together with "On the Essence of Ground," marks a main point of passage between *Being and Time* and *Contributions*. The relation between Dasein, death, and nothingness in its double sense, is thought again in *Contributions* in sections 201–202 where Heidegger rethinks the not-ground of Dasein as *"Wegsein,"* "being-away."

only disclosed in Dasein's anticipatory resoluteness, in an authentic existentiell mode of being. Meaning is defined by Heidegger as "that in which the intelligibility of something keeps itself, without coming into view explicitly and thematically. Meaning signifies that upon which (*woraufhin*) the primary project is projected, that in terms of which something can be conceived in its possibility as what it is" (BaT298; SuZ324). It follows that, as the meaning of care, temporality is that upon which Dasein is projected. Heidegger further explains that "to expose that upon which a project is projected, means to disclose what makes what is projected possible" (ibid.). In other words, that upon which Dasein is projected (temporality) is the condition of the possibility of the being of Dasein. The primary projection of which Heidegger speaks, the projection that first allows something to mean something, is the pre-theoretical understanding of being. In this projection the meaning not only of the being of Dasein but of all being of beings is disclosed.

Here, we see already pre-delineated how temporality (*Zeitlichkeit*) is the condition of the possibility not only for Dasein's own possibilities of being but also for the disclosure of being as such. But before developing this point further we need to consider how temporality occurs as that in terms of which we can conceive the possibility of Dasein's being (care).

Temporality is that which makes authentic being-a-whole of Dasein possible. It is constituted by three temporal ecstasies which correspond to the three existentials that constitute care. Resolute being-towards-death is only possible if Dasein can come back to itself in its ownmost, finite possibility of being and if this possibility of being is endured in Dasein's coming toward itself. In other words, Dasein's projection toward its most extreme possibility of being is grounded in a motion in which it comes toward itself. This *coming-towards-itself* is what Heidegger calls the original phenomenon of future;[13] it is the coming to be of Dasein in coming to itself. This first temporal ecstasy explains how Dasein occurs as an

---

13. "Coming-towards-itself" is the original phenomenon of future which occurs both in Dasein's authentic and inauthentic modes of being. Heidegger calls Dasein's authentic future, the ecstasy in which Dasein takes over its most extreme possibility of being (being-towards-death), "anticipation."

"always-already-having-transcended" out of which it comes back to its ownmost possibility of being.

In the taking over of thrownness Heidegger finds the second temporal ecstasy. Dasein can come toward itself only insofar as it *is* a having-been. Dasein can come toward itself only in *coming back toward* itself. Heidegger calls this coming back, Dasein's second temporal ecstasy, *"having-been"* (*Gewesenheit*). Having-been is constituted within the futural movement of Dasein's coming toward itself.[14]

The third and last ecstasy of temporality is *presencing* or "making present" (*Gegenwärtigen*) and occurs, again, at once with future and having-been. Presencing is the temporal meaning of being with beings, of letting be encountered what is grasped in action[15] (BaT 299f; SuZ 325f).

To the three ecstasies of temporality, which in their unity constitute the temporal meaning of the being of Dasein, there are three corresponding "horizons" or "horizonal schemata." In their unity, these three schemata form the temporal horizon of Dasein's temporal ecstasies, and thereby the meaning of being. However, within the preparatory analytic of Dasein in *Being and Time*, Heidegger develops the horizonal character of time only insofar as he shows how transcendence and being-in-the-world are founded in the ecstatic-horizonal temporality. Only later, in *The Basic Problems of Phenomenology*, does Heidegger show the way in which the horizon which is disclosed in Dasein's temporality is that from which being in general (*Sein überhaupt*) is understood, so that *in* the ecstatic-horizonal temporality of Dasein (*Zeitlichkeit*) a more originary horizonal temporality of being as such (*Temporalität*) is disclosed.

In section 69c of *Being and Time*, the horizonal character of Dasein's temporality is developed as the condition for the possibility of world. The horizon out of which world discloses in Dasein's thrown projection is articulated into three horizons or "horizonal schemata," which are the "toward which" of Dasein's three temporal ecstasies. The horizonal schemata delineate the horizon toward which the three ecstasies reach. This horizon is not a consequence of the temporal ecstasies but rather delim-

---

14. Authentic having-been in being-towards-death is called "retrieval" (*Wiederholung*).
15. Authentic presencing in anticipatory retrieving resoluteness is called "the moment" (*Augenblick*).

its and directs the ecstasies. In this sense, the horizonal schemata are not only the "whereto" of Dasein's ecstasies but also the "from-where." The schema of future in which Dasein comes toward itself is the "for-the-sake-of-itself"; the schema of having been is the "in the face of which" of thrownness; and the schema of presencing is the "in-order-to" (BaT333f; SuZ365).

In the light of Heidegger's analysis of guilt and being-towards-death, we can interpret the "for-the-sake-of-itself," which is the horizon of future out of which Dasein comes to itself, in its "nichthaft," its "not" quality. For-the-sake-of-itself means for the sake of Dasein's ownmost possibilities of being. This includes, with Dasein's originary limit (death), the possibility of not being. Thus, the "for-the-sake-of-itself" out of which Dasein's being discloses means also and originarily for the sake of Dasein's possibility of death, that possibility out of which its being is disclosed. We can relate this horizonal schema of future also to the other sense in which Dasein's possibilities of being carry a "not" quality. For-the-sake-of-itself means also for the sake of the not-ground that Dasein is as it projects itself onto determinate possibilities of being in the world with beings in which other possibilities remain excluded.

Similarly to the horizon of future, also the horizons of past and present delimit and open Dasein's being originarily in its "not" quality. The horizonal schema of having-been, the "in-the-face-of-which" of thrownness, originarily refers to being thrown into the possibility of not being as well as to being thrown into the exclusion of determinate possibilities of being. The schema of presencing, the in-order-to, is related to Dasein's not-ground in that it is the horizon out of which Dasein relates to beings in turning away from the possibilities of being and not being as such. In relating to things in the everyday taking care of things, Dasein does not face its ownmost possibilities of being and not being. Thus, the schema "in-order-to" enacts the original not-ground of Dasein by turning away from it.

The next and last step in the transcendental-horizonal itinerary of *Being and Time* shows the way in which being in general is disclosed in the horizonal schemata into which Dasein transcends in its temporal ecstasies. Said in another way, we must now see how being in general is disclosed in the horizonal schemata out of which Dasein temporalizes itself in transcending beings. In the book *Being and Time*, this last step of the project of fundamental ontology is not carried out. However, Heidegger partly develops it in *The Basic Problems of Phenomenology*. Since our concern is the project of fundamental ontology as a whole in distinction to Heidegger's approach to the question of being in *Contributions*, we need to take into account how Heidegger further develops the project of fundamental ontology in *The Basic Problems of Phenomenology*.

The bridge that, in *The Basic Problems of Phenomenology*, leads from the temporalizing of Dasein to horizonal temporality as the meaning of being as such is the pre-theoretical understanding of being that essentially belongs to Dasein. In order to show that, in the ecstatic-horizonal temporality of Dasein, being in general is disclosed, it suffices to show that the understanding of being, in which the being of beings in general is disclosed, is itself grounded in temporality. In *The Basic Problems of Phenomenology* Heidegger explains that to describe temporality insofar as it is the condition for the possibility of understanding being as such, he uses the term *Temporalität*, which we translate as *"horizonal temporality."* To show how the understanding of being is grounded in horizonal temporality, however, Heidegger does not need to go through all three of Dasein's temporal ecstasies. Because any one of them shows this, he limits his analysis to the explication of the temporal ecstasy of the present (*Gegenwart*) and its ecstatic horizon, presence (*Praesenz*) (BPP 306; GA 24, 435).

The horizonal schema of the "in-order-to" of Dasein's presencing (*Gegenwärtigen*) out of which Dasein relates to beings is rethought as presence. In Dasein's projection onto being as such, what is projected in Dasein's presencing is projected into the horizon of presence. The horizon of presence is that which schematically pre-delineates the whereto of the transcending projection in which being as such is disclosed, so that any being Dasein encounters is always already understood in terms of presence. Consequently, being at hand (*zuhanden*), being absent, or being objectively present (*vorhanden*) are all modes of presence. This means that in Dasein's opening projection, the being of beings in general is projected temporally out of the horizon of presence, i.e., out of horizonal temporality (BPP 307; GA24, 436). *"Therefore,"* Heidegger concludes, *"we understand being from the original horizonal schema of the ecstasies of temporality"* (ibid.).

In this last step of fundamental ontology two directions of thought and, with them, two ways of articulating this thought encroach each other. In the one direction, the temporal horizon through which being as such is disclosed is reached by delineating Dasein's transcendence into the temporal horizon of presence, future, and past. This direction determines the way in which Heidegger proceeds in *Being and Time*. In the other direction, the horizon into which Dasein transcends is thought to *pre-delineate* Dasein's transcendence and thus is understood as the *"from where"* of Dasein's transcendence.

The "into which" of Dasein's temporal ecstasies, the temporal horizon, is the "from where" of being's disclosure. The temporal horizon into which Dasein always already transcends is the delimiting origin that determines Dasein's thrown projection in which being as such is disclosed. Or, in Heidegger's own words from *The Basic Problems of Phenomenology:*

> temporality is intrinsically, original self-projection simply as such, so that wherever and whenever understanding exists [. . .], this understanding is possible only in temporality's self-projection. Temporality exists—*ist da*—as disclosed* because it makes possible the 'Da' [the "there"] and its disclosiveness in general. (BPP 307; GA24, 436f)

In making possible the disclosiveness of the "there," temporality is the "ground" of the disclosure of a world, of things in the world, and of Dasein as being-in-the-world. This ground is not anything permanent but rather is a temporal event. It is also not reducible to presence, since it discloses in its finitude, permeated by nothingness, in Dasein's authentic being-towards-death.

In *Contributions,* Heidegger rethinks the disclosive and finite character of the temporality that constitutes the meaning of being in *Being and Time* in the notion of *truth.* He unfolds truth as the unconcealing-concealment of being. But, as we will see, he does this in a way of thinking and saying which departs more radically from metaphysics.

b) Being and Time's *"Metaphysical" Approach*

It is now the moment to reflect in more detail on the extent to which the project of *Being and Time* is still "metaphysical" and the extent to which it goes beyond metaphysics. The following reflections arise in the light of the thinking of *Contributions;* they concern less "what" Heidegger wants to say in *Being and Time* and focus rather more on the motion of Heidegger's thinking as it develops in his project of fundamental ontology and in *our* thinking as we follow the transcendental-horizonal pathway in *Being and Time.*

1. We have seen how, in *Being and Time,* Heidegger approaches the question of being by way of an analysis of Dasein's transcendence into a temporal horizon in which being as such is disclosed. The articulation of the question of being in the perspective of Dasein's transcendence still draws from metaphysics, i.e., from a way of thinking which is representational and which departs from beings in order to inquire into their metaphysical ground, which is again represented analogously to beings as "beingness."[16] This is the case even if we take into account that Heidegger understands Dasein's transcending to originate in that toward which it is transcending. It remains to a certain extent metaphysical even if we understand the transcending of Dasein as an always-already-having-transcended and if we understand the "whereto" of Dasein's transcendence not as a highest being but as finite temporalizing event that is permeated by nothingness. Heidegger's approach to the question of being remains quasi-metaphysical because the notion of transcendence inevitably leads us to represent in our mind a motion which departs from a being (Dasein or ourselves) and leads to some other being (the temporal horizon), an other being that we analogously represent as an open horizon from which we come back to Dasein or ourselves, possibly in an "authentic" way. Similarly we tend to represent to ourselves the horizonal temporality and the projection of being onto time: we represent being as being-

16. When we conceive being analogously to beings, being is represented as something permanent and present; it is represented, in Heidegger's terminology, as "beingness," *Seiendheit.*

ness (as a kind of being) which projects itself onto a represented horizonal time in order to get from it its open occurrence. We thereby conceive the "ontological," i.e., being as such, in terms of the "ontic" (beings). As Heidegger says in section 262 of *Contributions:*

> We grasp the 'ontological' — even as condition for the 'ontic' — still only as an addendum to the ontic and repeat the 'ontological' (projecting-open a being onto beingness) once again as a self-application unto itself: projecting-opening beingness as projecting-opening of be-ing unto its truth. . . . By this approach be-ing itself is apparently still made into an object, and the most decisive opposite of that is attained which the course of the question of be-ing has already opened up for itself. (C317; B450f)

This means that even though we acknowledge a conceptual difference between being (as temporal event) and beings (as represented entities), we end up not really thinking being in its temporal meaning.

In its development, the project of fundamental ontology goes from a questioning of Dasein as the being that is interrogated (*Befragtes*) to a questioning of being as such and its horizonal time, i.e., what is asked about (*Erfragtes*). This project, which follows the path of a motion of transcendence, invites thinking to slip back into a metaphysical perspective that poses itself over against and therefore outside what it questions. This slippage occurs even if we conceptually understand the itinerary of *Being and Time* as one that leads back to its origin (horizonal time), and this origin as non-metaphysical in its finite, temporal quality. It may occur even if we try to remain attuned to an "authentic" disclosure of being in anticipatory resoluteness. The notions of transcendence and horizon do not arise out of the origin that they are meant to designate, but toward it.

One could say that this is "only" a problem of language, of conceptuality, but what is meant with these words goes beyond metaphysics, or is more originary. Such an explanation of the "failure" or rather incapability of saying being in *Being and Time* seems to make sense. The German word for "failure," "*Versagen,*" has the root meaning "saying" [-*sagen*] while the prefix "*ver-*" carries the sense of "against." Thus, "*Versagen*" itself suggests an inability to say, a failure of language. But if one is familiar with Heidegger's understanding of language from the thirties on, one hesitates to be satisfied with a simple distinction between metaphysical language and its non-metaphysical "content," as if the right meaning were already there and we needed only the correct words. Heidegger conceives of language as an articulation *of* being in the sense that being unfolds in language. Being is not something already there (an "other" to language) that words could represent and subsequently articulate. Being is an event that becomes manifest (or not) *in* words—if they are able to say it. And where, in a representational language, words suggest that being is something already there which words may or may not articulate, be-ing as a temporal occurrence withdraws "behind" these words and remains unsaid.[17] Consequently, the slippage to which the reader of *Being and Time* is subject, this slippage evoked by the transcendental-horizonal perspective of *Being and Time,* cannot be reversed as long as we use a representational language. The ability to articulate being withdraws in using the language of *Being and Time*—its language is not able adequately to say being. Following Heidegger's understanding of language, this is not a failure of the person Martin Heidegger; it is being in its historicality which gives itself to thought and, thus, this failure to say being is ultimately rooted in how being gives itself to thought in the project of *Being and Time.*

2. In addition to the notions of transcendence and horizon, the notion of "condition of the possibility"—in which Kant's transcendental philosophy resonates—also echoes a metaphysical way of thinking. The notion of "condition of the possibility" invites thinking to slip into a representational mode of thought in which thinking distances itself from what it says as it places itself over against what it wants to say. As we will see, the notion of a "condition of the possibility" also leads to a solidification of the ontological difference, and this, in turn, has consequences with respect to the role Dasein's facticity plays in fundamental ontology.

---

17. For a more detailed analysis of Heidegger's understanding of language and more specifically of the difference between a saying that discloses being and a language in which being withdraws ("propositional" or "representational" language) see Daniela Vallega-Neu, "Poietic Saying," in *Companion to Heidegger's "Contributions to Philosophy,"* ed. Charles E. Scott, Susan M. Schoenbohm, Daniela Vallega-Neu, and Alejandro Vallega (Bloomington and Indianapolis: Indiana University Press, 2001), especially pp. 67–70.

In the *Being and Time* project, horizonal time is articulated as the condition of the possibility of being's disclosure, ecstatic temporality is articulated as the condition of the possibility for Dasein's constitution as care, and being's disclosure in Dasein is articulated as the condition of the possibility for the discoveredness of beings. Besides evoking again the shadow of Kant's transcendental philosophy, the notion of "condition of the possibility" invites a return to metaphysical thinking simply because it is used in logic to define a causal connection: if not A then not B. When we think of such a connection, the motion of our thought leads us to separate in our mind the condition from what it conditions. With respect to the ontological difference between being and beings, for instance, being's disclosure remains separated from what it makes possible, namely, beings, and Dasein's facticity appears to remain separated from the disclosure of being as such. (Heidegger exposes the ontological structure of Dasein independently from its ontic occurrence.) And this occurs even if we consider that being and its temporal horizon disclose nowhere else than in Dasein's facticity, in the disclosive being-towards-death in anticipatory resoluteness.

In reading *Being and Time* one is easily led to represent to oneself an ontological structure that occurs at another level than the ontic-existentiell occurrence of Dasein, even when Heidegger points out that Dasein's being-a-whole needs an ontic attestation and that philosophical questioning needs to be grasped in an existentiell way. It is certainly possible, but far more difficult, to engage again and again in an understanding of the ontological dimension of being out of and within Dasein's "ontic" existence, out of an authentic, factual grasping of one's own being-towards-death in which being as such is disclosed out of a temporal occurrence. If we, as careful readers of *Being and Time,* were able to read this work by always authentically grasping our possibilities of being, allowing ourselves to be guided by an understanding of being that opens up in our existentiell activity of thoughtful reading, we would not consider the "ontological difference" as posing two "entities" but would rather understand this difference as a temporal occurrence, as a differencing that occurs in the motion of thinking, a differencing which also marks the slippage from openness of being to a representational encounter with beings, words, concepts.

Being and Time remains at once metaphysical and non-metaphysical. It is a work of transition, quasi-metaphysical in its language and revolutionary in its task. Probably it was necessary for Heidegger first to stretch traditional language to its limit before he could venture a "leap" into a different mode of thinking and speaking. As Heidegger says, *Being and Time* marks the "take-off for the leap" into another dimension of thinking, but it does not perform the leap itself (C162; B228).

In *Contributions,* Heidegger's critique of the transcendental approach to the question of being is severe. To think be-ing as such in its occurrence, as he says in section 110, "the representation of 'transcendence' in *every* sense must *disappear*" (C152; B217). In the same section he also says that the notion of "ontological difference"—as important as it first is to make visible the question of being as such in distinction to metaphysics as such—becomes the most decisive barrier to an understanding of be-ing. Thinking in terms of the ontological difference obstructs a more original understanding of being because it is a difference that originates in questioning beings as such (it originates in distinction to, i.e., with respect to metaphysics). Instead, what is required for a more original understanding of being is to find the more original unity of the ontological difference (a unity that resonates in the fact that fundamental ontology presupposes an ontic-existentiell opening of being).

> Therefore the task is not to surpass beings (transcendence) but rather to leap over this distinction and thus over *transcendence* and to inquire inceptually out of* be-ing and truth (*vom Seienden her und der Wahrheit*). (C177; B250)

The task is not to think *toward* the origin, toward the opening of being in its truth (temporality), but rather *from* the origin, from be-ing in its truth. This "turn" of thinking does not require just a new point of view—any talk of a point of view requires a viewer who is there at the outset and thus remains subjective. This turn of thinking requires a "leap," a letting go of any representational mode of thinking, of any supporting structure, value, or belief. Yet, according to Heidegger, this "letting go" cannot occur out of a free will—it is not an act of a subject—but must occur out of a necessity, out of a need which he understands as a historical event. This leads to the second realm of questioning which plays a major role in the transformative turn from fundamental ontology to be-ing-historical thinking: the more original insertion of thinking into the history of being.

2. THE MORE ORIGINARY
INSERTION INTO HISTORY

In our reading of *Being and Time* we have seen the way in which, for Heidegger, being discloses as such in Dasein's being-towards-death, how it discloses temporally in the possibility of not being. Being is thought, thus, in terms of a presencing out of a withdrawal. This motion of disclosive self-seclusion is what Heidegger in the thirties calls the *truth of be-ing* (*Wahrheit des Seyns*). One could say, then, that in *Being and Time* being discloses authentically for thinking in the enactment of Dasein's anticipatory resoluteness; it discloses factually in anxiety, in a fundamental attunement which unsettles thinking from its day-to-day engagement with things and from any representational mode of thinking. Thus, in order to be able to think being as such *as* it discloses "ontically" and "authentically" in anticipatory resoluteness, thinking needs to stay in this unsettled space; it needs to remain attuned to the "not" that permeates Dasein in its utmost and most original authentic possibility of being. This is precisely what Heidegger attempts to do in *Contributions*. Yet, in *Contributions*, this "not" finds a historical dimension. The "not"-being that permeates Dasein does not refer only to the possibility of the death of each human being, but opens up the history of be-ing, or, to be more precise, be-ing's historicality. Be-ing is no longer articulated, as in *Being and Time*, by means of an ontological structure which underlies history (in *Being and Time* Heidegger thinks history as being grounded in Dasein's temporality). Instead, be-ing itself opens as a historical occurrence, and thinking finds itself partaking in this occurrence, in this abysmal grounding in which a world opens historically. Heidegger calls this way of thinking "be-ing-historical thinking" (*seynsgeschichtliches Denken*).[1]

The more original insertion into the history of be-ing which marks

1. Sometimes Heidegger also writes *"seinsgeschichtliches Denken"* (being-historical thinking).

be-ing-historical thinking is twofold: First, it refers to a rethinking of the history of be-ing in its different epochs in our Western tradition *out of* and within the motion of the essential occurrence of the truth of be-ing. Second, it refers also to a transformation of thinking which no longer places itself, as it were, against the history of be-ing in the way in which it questions this history, but rather which finds itself caught up and determined by be-ing's historicality. By remaining in that grounding attunement that unsettles thinking from day-to-day life and representational thinking, be-ing-historical thinking finds itself historically enowned out of be-ing's occurrence, i.e., out of the truth of being. The truth of be-ing is thus thought as what Heidegger calls "enowning event" (*Ereignis*).

To develop further the more original insertion into history that marks the thinking of *Contributions*, that is, the thinking "from enowning," we first need to enter this work. The insertion into be-ing's historicality is discussed particularly in the third joining of *Contributions*, "The Leap." The godly (*das Gotthafte*), which marks the third thematic field that distinguishes fundamental ontology from be-ing-historical thinking in the questioning of be-ing as such, will be more explicitly discussed in the last joining of *Contributions*, "The Last God." But the questions of be-ing's historicality and of the godly permeate the entire work, i.e., all of the six joinings. As in a fugue, the different voices composing the piece belong together, so in *Contributions* the six joinings belong together in the saying of the truth of be-ing thought as enowning (*Ereignis*).

a) Contributions' *"Grand Fugue"*

In order to listen to the "grand fugue" of *Contributions*, we need among other things to learn the art of repetition; we need to learn to perform repetitions of movements of thinking in such a way that what is repeated occurs for us and with us each time anew. We also need to learn that what is repeated occurs only in the repetition, that it has no time, no space, no being outside of the repetition and, thus, occurs in a unique way each time. There is no truth of be-ing out there, standing by itself, which we could then think. There is no oneness of be-ing which we may or may not approach. Be-ing occurs in thinking as well as in other activities, and finds its uniqueness only there, each time anew, each time in a different way. We might think again of a musical piece. A musical composition is not music unless it is performed. Similarly, *Contributions* finds its life in a performative reading and listening which does not take the repetition of the same words or phrasings as mere repetitions of something which has already been thought or written down. Rather its life is in a reading and listening in which words open each time anew, and, in a unique way, in a time-space in which what gives itself to thought unfolds *as* it is thought. Heidegger calls such a thinking in which what is thought first comes to be *"er-denken,"* which in German usually means "to think something up." But since, for Heidegger, *"er-denken"* is rooted in be-ing and the prefix "er-" marks both the path character and the opening character of thinking, one may translate *"er-denken"* as "opening-thinking." Insofar as in this thinking what is thought unfolds and, thus, begins each time anew, this thinking is also called "inceptive," *"anfänglich."*

Heidegger calls the composition of *Contributions "Ge-füge"* or *"Fuge."* The German word *"Fuge"* means not only a musical fugue but also "joint," "seam," "cleft," or "fissure." Emad and Maly translate *"Fuge"* and *"Gefüge"* as "jointure," and *"Fügungen"* as "joinings." The "jointure" of *Contributions* is significantly different from a systematic work in the traditional sense, including—at least to a certain extent—*Being and Time.* The six joinings into which *Contributions* is divided do not present a systematic progression from one topic to the next in which one step would be the condition for the next. Rather, each joining addresses the whole jointure of *Contributions,* each joining addresses the same, but in a different way. As Heidegger says in section 39 of *Contributions:*

> In each of the six joinings the attempt is made always to say the same [*das Selbe*] of the same, but in each case from within another essential domain of that which enowning names. Seen externally and fragmentarily, one easily finds 'repetitions' everywhere. But what is most difficult is purely to enact in accord with the jointure, a persevering with the same, this witness of genuine inabiding of inceptual thinking. (C57; B81f)

The German word for "inabiding" is *"Inständlichkeit"* or *"Inständigkeit."*[2] With "in-abiding" Heidegger is rethinking Dasein's temporal "ecstasies" of *Being and Time*. But, as a consequence of the turning thematized earlier, the openness to being is no longer thought—transcendentally—as a "standing out" in the opening of being, but more inceptually as a "standing in" this opening. Therefore, the genuine *inabiding* of inceptual thinking means that thinking perseveres inceptually *in* the openness of the truth of be-ing and rethinks always anew, within this openness, this openness itself in different ways.

Inceptual thinking gets its name not only from this abiding in[3] the "same" (in the openness of being), unfolding it always anew, but, of course, also from the same which it thinks: the truth of be-ing as an inceptual, historical event. The inceptual thinking of *Contributions* is Heidegger's attempt to let the truth of be-ing itself direct thinking and to let its words emerge in the disclosure of truth. The root meaning of the German word for inceptual, *"anfänglich,"* is *"fangen,"* "to capture." The "-ceptual" of "inceptual" goes back to the Latin *"capere,"* which means to catch. Inceptual thinking is a thinking which, as it were, "catches" what is thrown to it. It "catches," or takes over, the "throw" (*Zuwurf*) of be-ing, and in doing so inceptually unfolds this throw. So, inceptual thinking is given to think the truth of be-ing by the truth of be-ing *as*[4] it thinks this truth. In other words, inceptual thinking finds itself enowned by the truth of be-ing *as* it (thinking) occurs. Consequently, the truth of be-ing is thought as enowning (*Ereignis*). Again: the truth of be-ing is thought as enowning because this is the way being occurs and is experienced *in* thinking if this thinking abides in the truth of be-ing. This implies that enowning does not occur separately from thinking but in and as it. In *Contributions*, the truth of be-ing unfolds as a jointure with six joinings *as* it is thought, but in such a way that thinking finds itself enowned by what it thinks. In other words, *Contributions*

2. Although "inabiding" is not a word used in current English, it translates as *"Inständlichkeit"* nicely because, as the German *"Inständlichkeit,"* "abiding" has the sense of persevering.
3. It appears redundant to me to use the expression "inabiding in," as does the Emad-Maly translation.
4. In this context, the adverb "as" renders nicely the "turning relation" (*kehriger Bezug*) in which enowning occurs.

owes its fugal composition, the joinings of its jointure, to "what" it attempts to think *while* what it thinks inceptually occurs in this thinking. *Contributions* owes its composition to the historical occurrence of the truth of be-ing *as* it unfolds in Heidegger's thinking.

What the essential subtitle of *Contributions to Philosophy*, *"From Enowning,"* tells us, then, is that *Contributions* does not say anything *about* the truth of be-ing, but rather that it enacts "a thinking-saying which is enowned by enowning and belongs to be-ing and to be-ing's word" (C3; B3). Here we can begin again to see how this way of thinking and saying differs considerably from the transcendental approach in *Being and Time*. In his earlier work, Heidegger questions being as such in its temporal character by thematizing Dasein's transcendence. In this approach, Dasein's transcending projection is taken as the first opening of being. In *Contributions*, this projection (*Ent-wurf*, i.e., literally "disclosive throw") is already thought as a response to a more originary throw, the throw (*Zuwurf*) or call (*Zuruf*) of being. In section 122 of *Contributions*, Heidegger makes clear that Dasein's projection opens the truth of be-ing only if it occurs out of the experience of being enowned, of being thrown through be-ing's enowning, and of belonging to be-ing. "That," says Heidegger, "is the essential difference from *every* [including *Being and Time's*] merely *transcendental* way of knowing with regard to the conditions of possibility" (C169; B239). One could say that in *Contributions*, unlike *Being and Time*, thrownness—in the sense of being enowned—now marks the first opening moment of the truth of be-ing. Of course, there is no truth of be-ing without both Dasein's thrownness and projection. More important, however, is that we understand that now thrown-projection is experienced and thought out of enowning. It is like awakening in the midst of an event, in the midst of a thinking which we experience as coming to us as we think. In these occurrences we feel as though we were witnessing an event, even though it seems we are performing it. Thinking is experienced as a *poietic* event, poietic in the way Heidegger translates the Greek word *"poiesis,"* namely in the sense of a *Hervorbringen*, a "bringing-forth."[5]

---

5. For Heidegger's translation of *poiesis*, see for instance his essay "The Question Concerning Technology," in *Basic Writings*, ed. David Farrell Krell (San Francisco: Harper-Collins, 1992), p. 317.

Accordingly, also the language in which this thinking is articulated is "poietic." It is not a language that thinking would choose deliberately in order to signify something that is already there. When and if a genuine thinking-saying "from enowning" succeeds, language emerges as an event of being that takes shape *as* thinking responds to and thus engages this event of being.

One could say, in an only indicative and preliminary way, that the transcending motion that was characteristic of *Being and Time* turns in *Contributions* into a motion of enownment belonging to the truth of be-ing. This turning implies a shifting or displacement, a *Ver-rückung* or *Ent-rückung* which transforms thinking and the way in which what is thought opens up in language. This is why Heidegger speaks of a "leap" into the truth of be-ing. With reference to such a leap, we might say that there is no smooth transition from *Being and Time* to *Contributions*, even if one acknowledges Heidegger's claim that be-ing has always been and remains the one question of his thinking, and even if one understands, with von Herrmann, the transformative turn from *Being and Time* to *Contributions* as an "immanent transformation" (*immanenter Wandel*).[6]

As indicated earlier, the transformation of thinking not only implies a shift in the way being is questioned and thus a shifting in the conceptuality and language of thinking, but also a deeper insertion into the historicality of be-ing. In the inceptual thought of *Contributions*, Heidegger understands the truth of be-ing as occurring in the transition from the first beginning to what he calls the other beginning of Western history. The truth of be-ing is experienced as an inceptual historical occurrence, but in a certain retention, in an undecidedness; being occurs in the in-between of what we may call, with Nietzsche, the death of the old god and the intimation of another beginning. In sections 5 and 6 of *Contributions*, Heidegger speaks of *intimation, Ahnung*, as a grounding attunement of being-historical thinking, which takes the place of the "wonder" which guided thinking in the first (Greek) beginning (C15; B20). It is this intimation of the other beginning which nourishes and guides the thinking of *Contributions*, even if thinking still experiences the shadow of the "old god" of

6. Friedrich-Wilhelm v. Herrmann, *Wege ins Ereignis. Zu Heidegger's 'Beiträge zur Philosophie'* (Frankfurt am Main: Klostermann, 1994), p. 30.

metaphysics. This is why Heidegger says in section 1 that the other beginning is always only intimated but yet is already decided, decided, we should add, in the inceptual opening thinking of *Contributions*. Historically, in a wider sense of "Western history," the other beginning is not yet decided,[7] and Heidegger regards *Contributions* as an attempt to prepare and hold open the time-space for such a historical decision. *Contributions* first traces out and brings into the open the transition to the other beginning of Western history, it attempts to prepare for the other beginning by providing a site for the truth of be-ing in Da-sein, in being-t/here.[8] The inceptual thought of *Contributions* does not find itself to be freely determined by the jointure of the truth of be-ing; enowning does not occur freely but holds itself back in a certain reserve. This reserve, however, is not a failure of thinking but is rather the way be-ing "gives itself" to thinking historically. This reserve and the transitory character of *Contributions* are reflected in the joinings of *Contributions* and in the way the truth of be-ing comes to language.

Before going to outline the six joinings which mark the composition of *Contributions* as a saying of the same, we should acknowledge another way in which *Contributions* differs considerably from any traditional systematic approach, including again, to a certain extent, *Being and Time*. Whereas a traditional systematic work aims at answering a question step by step, building one result on the other and ultimately presenting a complete system of thought, in *Contributions*, *questioning* remains the beginning and end of philosophical endeavor. The inceptive, transitional thought of *Contributions* is essentially a questioning because, as Heidegger says, the truth of be-ing is, and remains, what is most questionable and question-worthy (*das Fragwürdigste*).[9] The questioning is guided by that which is most question-worthy; it is essentially open to the event of be-ing, which in itself remains inexplicable, inexploitable in its abysmal

---

7. See for this particular questions the sections on "decision" in *Contributions*.
8. *Da-sein* is now written with a hyphen. In the following, *"Da-sein"* will be always translated as "being-t/here" in order to distinguish Da-sein from its use in *Being and Time* and also in order to avoid an understanding of Da-sein as some kind of being (*Seiendes*). For the meaning of being-t/here in *Contributions*, see sections 190 and 191.
9. *Contributions*, section 4.

and historical eventuating. *Contributions* is an open work, essentially unfinished, exploratory, and, at the same time, decided and rigorous in its pursuits. Its language carries at once delicacy and steadfastness, its vibrations dissipating in openness, with words which stand like Greek pillars in the middle of nothingness. *Contributions* achieves its peculiar work character,[10] its consistency (if we may use this expression), not by constructing a system on a firm base (there is also no *Befragtes* in *Contributions*), but through repeated questioning of the same (the truth of be-ing), through bringing forth in words, again and again, out of no-thing, be-ing as it historically occurs. One could perhaps say that *Contributions* occurs as a rhythmical abysmal thinking-saying. It is within this inceptual repetition of the same, which comes to be in questioning, that *Contributions* finds its articulation as six joinings. These joinings, says Heidegger in section 1, "are taken from the still unmastered ground plan of the historicity of the transition* itself" (C5; B6).[11] These joinings are named, in the Emad-Maly translation, "echo," "playing-forth," "leap," "grounding," "the ones to come," "the last god."

It is tempting to read these six joinings in a sequential way, as if they were different steps thinking takes from the first echo of be-ing to its crowning, the last god. It is also tempting to take one of the joinings and declare it the most important joining, the one from which all other joinings unfold. This has been done with "leap," "grounding," and "the last god."[12] Indeed, one probably can take any joining and develop from it the entire jointure of *Contributions* because, as Heidegger says, they all say the same—the truth of be-ing—but say it from a different essential

---

10. For the particular work character of *Contributions* in contrast to the traditional "system," see sections 1, 28, 39, 43 (C5, 45f, 56f, 61f; B5, 65, 81f, 88f).

11. "Transition" is a more literal translation of the German word *"Übergang"* than is "crossing," which is the word used in the Emad-Maly translation.

12. George Kovacs, "The Leap for Being in Heidegger's *Beiträge zur Philosophie (Vom Ereignis),"* Man and World 25 (1992): 39–59; William J. Richardson, "Dasein and the Ground of Negativity: A Note on the Fourth Movement in the *Beiträge*-Symphony," *Heidegger Studies* 9 (1993): 35–52; Günter Figal, "Forgetfulness of God: Concerning the Center of Heidegger's *Contributions to Philosophy,"* in *Companion to Heidegger's "Contributions to Philosophy,"* ed. Charles E. Scott, Susan M. Schoenbohm, Daniela Vallega-Neu, and Alejandro Vallega (Bloomington and Indianapolis: Indiana University Press, 2001), pp. 196–212.

domain of its swaying (C57; B81f). Each joining is intrinsically joined to the others out of a common "grounding attunement," which Heidegger calls mostly *Verhaltenheit*, in the Emad-Maly translation, "reserved-ness." At the same time, all joinings have specific guiding attunements; each part of the fugue having its specific "sound" which resounds in the grounding attunement of the whole fugue or jointure. In section 5, Heidegger points out that the grounding attunement "vibrates in differ-ent guiding attunements," in startled dismay, reservedness, and awe. Heidegger considers these guiding attunements explicitly at the begin-ning of each section that opens a new joining, and we, as readers, are in-vited to let our own reading be guided by them. This is why it makes sense to introduce the following short presentation of the six joinings of *Contributions* by means of an exposition of these guiding attunements.[13]

The guiding attunement of "Echo," the first joining, is, as Heidegger says in the opening section 50, *Schrecken* and *Scheu*, i.e., "startled dis-may,"[14] together with awe*.[15] Both emerge from the grounding attune-ment of reservedness. In startled dismay, thinking is "set out"[16] from what is familiar and acknowledges the distress of what Heidegger calls the "abandonment of be-ing" (*Seinsverlassenheit*). Thinking acknowledges that be-ing has abandoned beings in the domination of what Heidegger calls machination (*Machenschaft*). Machination denotes a mode of being which characterizes our present epoch, and which tends to exhaust the oc-currence of be-ing in the makeability of things; beings, things, are reduced to mere exchangeable products of calculative thinking. The domination of machination tends to close the very possibility of a more originary occur-rence and experience of be-ing and thus evokes the distress of the aban-donment of be-ing if this abandonment is experienced as such. The Ger-man word which "awe"[17] is an attempt to translate is "*Scheu*," which

13. For a more detailed discussion of the six joinings, see the second part of this book.
14. I understand "*Schrecken*" to mean the same as "*Erschrecken*" in section 5.
15. I do not see the need to speak of "deep awe" as the Emad-Maly translation does.
16. In German, to be set out, "*ent-setzt sein,*" also means to be horrified; thus "*Ent-setzen*" is close to the guiding attunement "startled dismay" (*Erschrecken*). In section 269 of *Con-tributions*, Heidegger calls it "the originary rift of what has the character of tuning itself. The grounding-attunement of anxiety sustains the setting out* [. . .]" (C340; B483).
17. A connotation of the English word "awe" which is not present in the German "*Scheu*" is that of a reverentiality.

usually means "shyness." A delicate silence and hesitation that belong to shyness also play in the guiding attunement of "Echo," in which an unsettling rift (opened in the experience of the abandonment of being) is attended with a delicate silence and hesitation. The experience of the abandonment of being is acknowledged and held open if thinking is not only attuned by startled dismay but at the same time by a hesitant awe before what opens up in the experience of the abandonment of be-ing. What opens up is an "echo" or reverberation of be-ing in its withdrawal. Thus, thinking experiences that be-ing occurs as this withdrawal, which is accompanied by a compelling distress (*nötigende Not*), a need to let be-ing occur historically. "Echo," says Heidegger in section 50, "must encompass the whole of the rift and above all be articulated as the mirroring of playing-forth" (C75; B107). The "whole of the rift" means the whole of the jointure of *Contributions* in its articulation into six joinings, which is taken from the historicality of be-ing itself in the transition from the first to the other beginning of history. The echo of be-ing opens up be-ing's historicality in-between the ending of the first beginning and the intimation of the other beginning of history. The relation between the first and the other beginning is explored especially in the next joining, "Playing-forth."

In section 81, Heidegger calls the guiding attunement of "Playing-forth" the "delight in alternately surpassing the beginnings in questioning" (C119; B169). The beginnings in question are the first and the other beginning of Western history. These beginnings are not separate but are thought in relation to each other; the thought of the one arises in relation to the other. The other beginning, the beginning which *Contributions* attempts to prepare, is thought in a reawakening, a rethinking of the first beginning of Western thought in ancient Greece and of its completion in the present era of technology, as well as in Nietzsche's philosophy. In this reawakening, the first beginning is brought into a decisive encounter (*Auseinandersetzung*) with the other. The playing-forth in-between the beginnings is intimately related to the echo of be-ing, the echo of be-ing's occurrence as withdrawal. The echo of be-ing is thought as a historical event which carries both the abandonment of be-ing initiated in the first beginning (where the occurrence of be-ing as withdrawal is covered up by a questioning of beings) and the necessity of bringing the essential occurrence of the truth of be-ing again into the openness of history. This would occur in the "grounding" of the other beginning. The distress which is experienced and acknowledged in the echo of be-ing is in itself compelling; it is a *"nötigende Not,"* a "compelling distress" which compels thinking to prepare the "grounds," i.e., the site and moment for the possibility of another beginning. This possibility is continuously reinforced by rethinking again and again the meaning of the Greek word *phusis*, which for Heidegger names an overpowering (*übermächtig*) event of be-ing which has determined more than two thousand years of Western history.

As thinking engages in the compelling distress of be-ing (which arises as thinking experiences be-ing's withdrawal and rethinks the first beginning of Western history), the third joining, the "Leap," joins the jointure of the truth of be-ing in the transition from the first to the other beginning. The leap is, according to Heidegger, "the most daring move in the proceeding of*[18] inceptual thinking." It "abandons and throws aside everything familiar" and leaps into "belongingness to be-ing in its full essential swaying as enowning" (Section 115, C161; B227). For Heidegger, "the leap is to dare an initial foray into the domain of the *history of be-ing* [*Seinsgeschichte*]*" (ibid.). To leap into the truth of be-ing does not reside in the will of a courageous subject. As we noted earlier, it arises, rather, in the guiding attunement of awe (in a silent reserve) out of the compelling distress of be-ing's withdrawal in the playing-forth of the first and the other beginning. In the leap, thinking leaps into the truth of be-ing that is opened up transitionally in the first two joinings. But it also brings about "belongingness to be-ing in its full essential swaying." The "essential swaying" (*Wesung*) of be-ing here names the originary event of be-ing, when be-ing discloses originarily as enowning.[19] As Heidegger says in sec-

18. The German states *"im Vorgehen des anfänglichen Denkens."* To translate *"des"* as "from" introduces a direction of thought into the text that is not there in the German. Had Heidegger intended to say "from inceptual thinking," he would have written *"im Vorgehen vom anfänglichen Denken her."* We should also keep in mind that inceptual thinking proceeds from the event of be-ing and not from "itself."

19. "Essential swaying" is an attempt to translate the German *"Wesung."* The word *"Wesung"* is not used in colloquial German but it resonates both with *"Verwesung"* (which means "decay," for instance of plants or corpses) and with *"Wesen"* ("essence," which Heidegger rethinks in a verbal sense). Thus, *"Wesung"* points to the temporality of "life," to the coming to be and passing away inherent to be-ing. One may translate *"Wesung"* also

tion 5, awe "gives rise to the necessity of reticence" that is "the letting-hold-sway of be-ing as enowning" (C12; B15f). Compared to the startled dismay which guides the first joining, the guiding attunement of awe characterizes the belonging to and letting be of the realm into which thinking is set out, once it has acknowledged the abandonment of being out of be-ing's occurrence as withdrawal. The realm of the history of be-ing, which is opened up in the leap, is the realm of be-ing's occurring as enowning. In the leap, thinking experiences its own enownment as it thinks what gives itself to thinking. Here thinking finds itself belonging and answering to (ent-sprechen) the call of be-ing, it finds itself being summoned to think of be-ing, which arises in the compelling distress of the abandonment of be-ing. Thinking finds itself responding historically to be-ing's summons in grounding a time-space for the disclosure of the truth of be-ing, the Augenblicksstätte (the site of the moment) in which, eventually, the other beginning of Western history may or may not take its course.

The leap is intimately connected with the fourth joining, "Grounding." In section 187 of Contributions, Heidegger points out that grounding has a twofold meaning. The first and original meaning relates to the truth of be-ing which occurs as an abysmal* grounding. It is abysmal because be-ing occurs as a withdrawal; it also "grounds" in the sense that out of the withdrawal a compelling summons arises to ground a historical time-space in being-t/here. The second meaning of grounding refers to the way in which the original ground (ground in the first sense) is reached and taken over in being-t/here. This second meaning is the one that is especially relevant to the leap since, as Heidegger says, in the leap, the truth of be-ing is "taken over." This "taking over" of the truth of be-ing indicates Dasein's "response" to the compelling summons of be-ing. In this second sense of grounding, Heidegger speaks of er-gründen,[20] which usually means "to fathom," in the sense of "to get to the bottom of, compre-

---

as "essential occurrence." For the similarity and difference between "Wesen" ("essence," "essential sway") and "Wesung," see Contributions, translators' "Foreword," pp. xxiv–xxvii.

20. Emad and Maly translate "er-gründen" as "en-grounding." For the different meanings of the German prefix "er-" which play in "er-gründen," see Contributions, the translators' Foreword, p. xxxvii.

hend something." This meaning certainly resonates in what Heidegger means by *er-gründen*. But *er-gründen* has a more literal sense in *Contributions;* with this word Heidegger rethinks Dasein's projection in *Being and Time*, but now as response to the abysmal grounding event of be-ing, as a response which at the same time discloses the truth of be-ing as an abysmal event. In the following, *er-gründen* is translated as "projecting-grounding.*"

The twofold meaning of grounding, grounding as being's abysmal event and grounding in the sense of projecting-grounding, reflects what Heidegger calls the turning in enowning (*Kehre des Ereignisses*). This turning occurs in-between the truth of be-ing. One could also say that the truth of be-ing occurs as the expansion of this in-between; it occurs in-between the enowning call of be-ing and the enowned belonging response in being-t/here (*Da-sein*). But, in this turning between the call of be-ing and being-t/here's response, being-t/here is not thought in opposition to or over against the call of be-ing, nor does it primarily refer to human being. Rather, being-t/here names the in-between, the "point of turning" (*Wendungspunkt*) or the opening in the turning of enowning (C, sections 190 and 191).

Being-t/here opens up the essential occurrence of the truth of be-ing if this truth is reached in the leap and held open while abiding in this truth. This, for Heidegger, requires humans. The fact that Heidegger reintroduces into his thought the word "human" (in distinction to *Da-sein*) does not mean that humans are thought primarily as beings. As it is the case with Dasein in *Being and Time*, the humans of which Heidegger speaks in *Contributions* are thought primarily in their *being*—in fact, in their authentic way of being—which is the being of being-t/here (Da-sein). Attuned through reservedness, humans abide in the "t/here," they *are* (*-sein*) the "t/here" (*Da-*) of being-t/here (*Da-sein*).[21] They abide in the opening of the truth of be-ing by remaining attuned to this opening, i.e., to being's enowning withdrawal, and by sheltering it in a being (for instance, words, works of art, gestures). Abiding in being-t/here, sheltering the

---

21. We see here again how the notion of "abiding in,"* "*Inständigkeit*," replaces the notion of Da-sein's ecstasies in *Being and Time*.

truth of be-ing in beings, humans first come to be who they essentially are: "seekers," "preservers," and "guardians" of the truth of be-ing. These three determinations reflect the three temporal ecstasies of Dasein in *Being and Time:* future, having been, and presencing.[22]

Those humans who truly belong to the truth of be-ing in being "seekers," "preservers," and "guardians" are grounders of this truth. Heidegger calls them also "the ones to come." Again, we have moved into the next joining of the jointure of *Contributions*. The ones to come are so named not just because they are not yet. To a certain extent Heidegger would count at least himself and Hölderlin among "the ones to come." The ones to come, *die Zu-künftigen,* get their name in relation to the gods in that they are the ones to whom the "hint and onset of distancing and nearing of the last god" comes (C277; B395). The ones to come are attuned not only by a guiding attunement (*Leitstimmung*) but by the grounding attunement (*Grundstimmung*) of "reservedness" which discloses being inceptively and in which all the different guiding attunements (startled dismay, awe) are gathered. An endurance and a holding oneself back reverberate in the word "reservedness" (*Verhaltenheit*). Reservedness attunes to be-ing's disclosure as withdrawal and enowning event; it allows humans to abide in this inceptive, abysmal opening and to not turn away from it. In reservedness, humans withstand be-ing's occurrence as withdrawal while allowing this occurrence to happen. In this way, humans allow the truth of be-ing to occur not only as withdrawal but as an enowning event in which they come to be who they are in relation to the gods. The moment when be-ing in its truth occurs as enowning (and not only as withdrawal like in metaphysics) marks also the beginning of the (not yet fully unfolded) other beginning of Western history. The ones to come, who are attuned by reservedness, are grounders of the truth of be-ing in that they open the possibility of a decision over the other beginning of history.

The ones to come are intimately related to "the passing of the last god." Being-t/here is the turning point, the in-between not only for the enowning call of be-ing and the enowned belonging to be-ing, but also for the in-between of humans (as grounders) and of gods (and their history). In Da-

22. For a more detailed discussion of this relation, see Chapter 6, b) of this book.

sein, humans and gods are brought to a decisive encounter (C331; B470, section 267).

Heidegger says that the last god has nothing to do with a Christian god or any kind of being (*Seiendes*). He speaks of the last god not as an entity but rather of its (the god's) occurrence in an event. The last god occurs in its passing, in a passage (*Vorbeigang*) which marks the decision of the other beginning of history. "*Last*" here has both the meaning of that which is "the longest fore-runnership" (*Vorläuferschaft*) and of the "deepest beginning," as Heidegger says in the opening section 253 of the last joining of *Contributions*. In *Contributions*, the last god gives itself to thought not yet in the event of its passing but still *in* this "not yet" in a *hint:* "The last god has its *essential swaying* [*Wesung*] within the hint, the onset and staying-away of the arrival as well as the flight of the gods who have been, and within their concealed* [*verborgenen*] transformation" (C288; B409).[23] The hint of the last god gathers an undecidedness regarding the onset (*Anfall*) or staying away (*Ausbleib*) and the arrival or flight of the gods.[24] It gathers the temporality of coming and leaving, which, in the transition from the first to the other beginning of Western history, remains undecided. The hint of the last god, a hint which bears at the same time both its most remote distance (in the flight) and unique nearness (in the arrival), re-sounds already in the echo of the truth of be-ing. The nearness of the last god, says Heidegger, "echoes in the echo of be-ing out of the experience of distress of abandonment by being" (C290; B412). We could say, then, that the hint of the last god echoes out of the compelling distress in the experience of the utmost abandonment of be-ing. This abandonment goes along with the flight of the gods but at the same time bears the possibility of the arrival of the gods out of the compelling summons, which arises in the abandonment of being, to ground a time-space for the truth of be-ing in which the passing of the last god could occur. The appearance of the last

23. "*Verborgen*" means in the first place "concealed," in the sense of not being exposed or visible. Emad and Maly translate "*verborgen*" as "sheltered and hidden" in order to explicate a sheltering (*bergen*) involved in this being concealed. However, this sheltering, which is at play in "*verbergen*," occurs differently than the sheltering of which Heidegger speaks more explicitly in *Contributions*. Here, sheltering refers to the way in which the truth of being finds a historical site, i.e., an opening through beings which shelter this truth.
24. For the relation between the "last god" and the "gods," see Chapter 8 of this book.

god in its passing would determine the other beginning of Western history, another beginning which, in the transitional thought of *Contributions,* is in the process of decision but is as yet undecided with respect to its epochal occurrence. The undecidedness in the opening of the decision of be-ing's historicality is indicated in the undecidedness regarding the onset or staying away and the arrival or flight of the gods.

The compelling distress of the abandonment of being unfolds in *Contributions* as the distress of the gods. In section 267 of the last part of *Contributions,* "Das Seyn," Heidegger attempts a thinking-saying from enowning which says together the manifoldness of occurrences in which enowning occurs. In this section, Heidegger says that Da-sein is enowned through (*durch,* not "by") the gods, out of the gods' need of be-ing (C331; B470). This does not mean that the gods are the ones who enown being-t/here. In this case one would place the gods over be-ing and conceive them as some kind of entities that would "create" being. But Heidegger does not think of the gods as creators, nor does he think of them as being. Indeed, the gods, Heidegger says, essentially "are" not (they occur not yet and not any more), and out of their not-being, they give themselves to thought as needing be-ing and therefore as needing humans as the grounders of the truth of be-ing. The gods need humans as the grounders of the time-space, of the site of the moment (*Augenblicksstätte*) in which the last god may appear in its passing and thereby inaugurate a new beginning of history.

In *Contributions,* gods and humans are thought inceptually as emerging in enowning in their separateness but also in their mutual belonging. They are thought out of being-t/here as they emerge in the thinking of *Contributions* in transition from metaphysics to another beginning of history. Attuned by reservedness, thinking hesitantly holds open be-ing's withdrawal as it answers a hint that is announced most remotely in the acknowledged experience of the utmost abandonment of being in beings.

b) Being and Time *in the Context of* Contributions

The sixfold jointure of the truth of be-ing that emerges in *Contributions* is Heidegger's attempt to think from enowning, i.e., to bring to language, to words, and consequently into the openness of history an event which gives itself to thinking *as* thinking inceptively projects that event. This event is the essential occurrence of the truth of be-ing in the transition from the first to the other beginning. The transition occurs as a decision concerning be-ing's historicality, namely whether be-ing will definitively withdraw in the domination of machination or whether be-ing will grant another beginning of history. In what follows, we will reflect once again back on *Being and Time* and see how we can understand this first major work of Heidegger in the context of the essential character and peculiar jointure of *Contributions* unfolded in the previous section.

In section 117 of *Contributions*, Heidegger explicitly understands the fundamental ontology of *Being and Time* as the "*transition* from the end of the first to the other beginning." But the transition, he says, "is at the same time the take-off for the leap" by which alone the other beginning can begin (C162; B228f). We could say, then, that *Being and Time* already moves in the joinings of echo and playing-forth. This work is already compelled by the abandonment of being, that is, by be-ing's withdrawal from beings, as Heidegger says retrospectively. Yet the thinking in *Being and Time* does not perform the leap into the belongingness to be-ing; it does not attempt to speak "from enowning." Crucial for a thinking and saying from and of enowning is the attunement to be-ing. This means more specifically that a thinking and saying speak within and out of the disclosing power of a grounding attunement to be-ing and its withdrawal. An insight into the disclosive power of a grounding attunement, which authentically opens up the occurrence of be-ing as such, is already present in *Being and Time*. In this work, Heidegger thinks of anxiety as the grounding attunement that displaces Dasein from every-dayness and opens not only the being of Dasein as a whole but also being as such. He also finds, as we have seen, the ontic attestation for an existentiell opening of be-ing as such in the call of conscience, a call which emerges in anxiety out of the "not-ground" that Dasein is in its utmost possibility of not-being, in its being-towards-death. The call comes suddenly out of Dasein and yet over Dasein, and calls Dasein back to the not-ground that it is. As Heidegger says, "The call comes from afar to afar. It reaches him who wants to be brought back"

(BaT251; SuZ271). In listening and responding to this call, Dasein exists authentically and takes over its most authentic possibility of being.

We thus readily see the similarity of the call of conscience to the call of be-ing which echoes out of be-ing's withdrawal, out of the abysmal opening of be-ing. In section 202 of *Contributions*, Heidegger points directly to the relation between Da-sein, death (being-away), and being in its withdrawal (nothingness) when he says:

> "As the utmost of the t/here (*Da*), death is at the same time the core of its possibly total transformation. And therein lies at the same time the allusion to the deepest sway of the nothing" ("nothing" here understood as be-ing in its withdrawal).[25] "What here as ownmost shelteredness-concealedness advances into the t/here (*Da*)—the reciprocal relation of the t/here [*Da*] to the away [*death*] that is turned toward the t/here (*Da*)—is the mirroring of the turning in the essential sway of being itself [the mirroring of the turning in enowning]. The more originarily being is experienced in its truth, the deeper is the *nothing* as the abyss* at the edge of the ground." (C228; B325)

Here, Heidegger indicates that death is an "allusion," an indication of the withdrawal as which be-ing occurs. The disclosure of Dasein's ownmost possibilities of being out of its possibility of death is thought in relation to the disclosive enowning that occurs in be-ing's withdrawal. We can say, then, retrospectively, that the relation of Da-sein to its death, i.e., being away, which Heidegger unfolds in *Being and Time*, mirrors the turning in enowning that he unfolds in *Contributions*. Except that in *Contributions*, thinking performs the "leap" into the truth of be-ing by holding itself in the grounding attunement of reservedness, and, so, holds itself authentically in relation to the "nothingness," "the withdrawal of be-ing" which discloses in anticipatory resoluteness. Compared to the conceptuality of *Being and Time*, one could say that in *Contributions*, thinking is performed in an existentiell authentic mode of being. In anticipatory resoluteness, thinking remains attuned to and acknowledges the possibility of its death, and, in this openness to death (to being-away), the truth of be-ing resounds as enowning withdrawal.

25. See section 145 of *Contributions*.

In *Being and Time,* authentic being in anticipatory resoluteness allows the philosopher to experience and question being as such rather than merely question beings in their being. But at the same time, in the transcendental approach to the question of being, thinking tends to slide away from its authentic opening to being and to think being with reference to beings.[26] One could understand the ontological difference as a reflection Heidegger makes on this move: a move from an authentic opening of being to a representational approach to beings. This is mirrored in the fact that in *Being and Time,* Dasein is conceived both as a being (an entity) that encounters other beings, and, primarily and more originarily, as a projecting open in a motion of transcendence out of its openness to being as such, back to the presencing of beings. Thus Dasein's motion of transcendence occurs as the motion of the ontological difference.

In *Contributions,* Heidegger departs from a thinking in terms of the ontological difference which still places the thinking of fundamental ontology in an ambiguous position as it slides back and forth from an authentic mode of being to a representational mode of thinking. In be-ing-historical thinking, the difference between be-ing and beings is thought from within the openness of be-ing, out of an authentic mode of being (to use the language of *Being and Time*), or, at least, we should say that Heidegger attempts to think in such a way. In *Contributions,* beings are not thought in opposition to the opening of be-ing but rather as essential constituents for the occurrence of this truth. In order to occur historically and inceptually, the truth of be-ing needs to find a site, a time-space in being-t/here. But Heidegger says that in order to keep this site open as a site where truth happens historically, truth needs to be sheltered in a being. Without beings there is no being-t/here and thus no historical time-space for the truth of be-ing. Heidegger has elaborated this relation in greater detail in his essay "The Origin of the Work of Art."[27] In this essay, which should be considered as an essential complement to *Contributions,* Heidegger attempts to think the way in which a being (a work of art) can keep disclosed being-t/here so that the truth of be-ing can shine forth inceptually.

26. See Chapter 1, b) of this book, which elaborates this point.
27. In Martin Heidegger, *Basic Writings.*

In *Contributions*, Heidegger does not only think of this inceptual sheltering as something that needs to occur in a future which would mark the beginning of a new epoch of Western history; he attempts to perform this inceptual sheltering "himself" in his thinking and saying "from enowning." The words of *Contributions* are an attempt to shelter the truth of being in being-t/here, to bring into the open of history the transition from the first to the other beginning as it gives itself to thinking. Accordingly, Heidegger not only tries to think the difference between being and beings in their originary unity, but he attempts to perform this originary unity in his thinking. To be more precise, for Heidegger the originary unity of being and beings can be thought adequately only if it is also *performed*, that is, enacted in thinking saying. This is a decidedly different approach to thinking from *Being and Time*. Heidegger's thinking becomes be-ing-historical and ceases to be transcendental in his attempt to respond to the compelling necessity of grounding the truth of be-ing in Da-sein out of the experience of the abandonment of be-ing. *Contributions* attempts to *perform* what it thinks, or, maybe one should rather say, to think what emerges in its performing as "something" which gives itself to thought, i.e., which enowns thinking.

Several determinations (*Bestimmungen*) arise in the be-ing-historical thinking of *Contributions* as it responds to be-ing's enowning call. These determinations concern humans and gods, world and earth, beings in their truth, and Western history. Looking back again at *Being and Time* with reference to *Contributions*, we could say that in the call of conscience far more arises than Dasein's *vorrufender Rückruf*, the call which calls Dasein ahead and back to its ownmost possibility of being the not-ground that it originarily is. The enownment of the authentic self of Dasein is "only" one determination that arises in *Contributions*. In section 197 of *Contributions*, Heidegger rethinks the authentic self of Dasein out of enowning as the "enowned belonging" to the truth of be-ing, a truth, of course, which opens up in its abysmal character in be-ing's withdrawal, a truth, therefore, that occurs as not-ground. In the enownment of Dasein's selfhood, humans are enowned to hold open the truth of be-ing by being "seekers," "preservers," and "guardians" of this truth. This ownmost being of humans occurs in manifold ways of sheltering truth in words, works of art, deeds, etc., by abiding in the truth of be-ing out of the grounding attunement of reservedness.

The other determinations which arise in the enowned thought of *Contributions* point again to the second and third thematic fields which mark a difference between *Being and Time* and *Contributions*, namely (1) the deeper insertion of thinking into history and (2) the dimension of the godly. One could say that out of the lack that the call of conscience in *Being and Time* gives to understand, there comes, in *Contributions*, word of a decision over the destiny of Western history, as well as the hint of an event which Heidegger calls the passing of the last god. These determinations (the decision over Western history and the passing of the last god) arise within the context of Heidegger's readings, especially of the Presocratics (the first beginning), of Nietzsche (the completion of the first beginning in its closure), and of Hölderlin (the intimation of another beginning).

The opening of the decision concerning the destiny of Western history adduced in *Contributions* is more than analogous to the decision Dasein takes in anticipatory resoluteness adduced in *Being and Time*. In the decision of Dasein (in *Being and Time*), Dasein chooses to take over and to remain exposed to the double not-ground that it is, i.e., to the possibility of its own impossibility (death) and the closure of determinate possibilities of being in the choice of others. In *Contributions*, the originary being a not-ground of Dasein (which in *Being and Time* is Dasein's own death) bears epochal dimensions: It mirrors the possibility of the closure of the history of be-ing, which, as it opens up, discloses the originary swaying of be-ing as a beginning of history. Thus, the decision concerning one's authentic self turns into a decision concerning the history of be-ing. Our authentic being becomes dependent upon or grounded in the decision over the possibility or impossibility of another beginning of Western history.

Heidegger considers the occurrence of be-ing as a beginning of history, especially as he rereads the Presocratics in the light of be-ing's occurrence as opening withdrawal. In addition, he thinks the possibility of the impossibility of be-ing, especially through his reading of Nietzsche as the one who completes (*vollendet*) the first beginning. Finally, it is Hölderlin who, for Heidegger, first announces the possibility of another beginning in the experience of the flight of the old (Greek) gods.

Hölderlin is the one who influences most Heidegger's thinking of the dimension of the godly as it plays into the thinking "from enowning." To pick up again the choice of Dasein's authentic self in *Being and Time,* this authentic self is not only grounded in the history of be-ing but also depends upon the enownment of the gods. According to Heidegger, we humans come to be who we are essentially in the encounter (*Ent-gegnung*) with the gods, since it is their need to be, their need for a site of be-ing (being-t/here) which compels humans to abide in being-t/here and thence to provide a historical site and moment for the truth of be-ing as withdrawal. "'Gods' need be-ing in order through be-ing—which does not belong to gods—nevertheless to belong to themselves" (C309; B438).

The call of conscience of which Heidegger speaks in *Being and Time* is thought to be rooted, in *Contributions,* in the need of the gods. The gods' need to be calls humans back to the not-ground out of which they come to be who they are; it calls humans to endure be-ing's withdrawal in order to ground a moment and site (being-t/here) for the history of be-ing. This means that another history of be-ing emerges only in response to the need of the gods.[28] That being the case, the decision of the other beginning of history is intimately connected with the decision over the arrival or flight of the gods. These connections will be explored further in the second part of this book. Since the aim of this part of the present introduction to Heidegger's *Contributions* is above all the discussion of *Contributions* in the context of *Being and Time,* we will end it here in order to give way to a more detailed exposition of the six joinings of *Contributions.*

---

28. This is the context of Heidegger's famous saying in the Spiegel interview: "Only a god can still save us." In *Martin Heidegger and National Socialism: Questions and Answers,* ed. Günter Neske and Emil Kettering (New York: Paragon House, 1990), p.57.

PART TWO

The Six Joinings of *Contributions*

In section 39 of *Contributions*, Heidegger describes the internal connection and unity of the six joinings that compose this second major work:

> Every joining stands for itself, and yet there is a hidden inter-resonating and an opening* grounding of the site of decision for the essential transition* into the still possible transformation of Western history.
> *Echo* carries far into what has been and what is to come—hence in and through the playing-forth its striking power on the present.
> *Playing-forth* receives its necessity primarily from the echo of the distress of the abandonment of being.
> Echo and playing-forth are the soil and field for inceptual thinking's first leaping off for *leaping* into the essential swaying of be-ing.
> The leap first of all opens up the ungone expanses and concealments of that into which the *grounding* of being-*t/here**, which belongs to the call of enowning, must press forth.
> All of these joinings must be sustained in such a unity*, from within the abiding in being-*t/*here*, which distinguishes the being of *those who are to come*.
> I hose who are to come take over and preserve belongingness to enowning and its turning, a belongingness that has been awakened by the call. They come thus to stand before the hints of the *last god*. (C57; B82)

As we follow Heidegger through the six joinings of *Contributions*, we should keep in mind that they are not meant to designate different events in a linear time sequence. Rather, they name the way in which being as enowning opens up for thinking in the transition from metaphysics to another realm of questioning.[1]

---

1. For the guiding attunements of each of the joinings, see the previous section, "*Contributions*' 'Grand Fugue'" (Chapter 2a).

3. ECHO

The concepts which dominate the first joining of *Contributions* are *"Anklang"* (Echo), *"Seinsverlassenheit"* (Abandonment of Being), *"Seinsvergessenheit"* (Forgottenness of Being),[1] *"Machenschaft"* (Machination), *"Erlebnis"* (Lived Experience), *"das Riesenhafte"* (the Gigantic), and considerations regarding *modern science*. Of course all these concepts belong intimately together. They mark different aspects of the same occurrence, the occurrence that resonates in the echo of the essential swaying of be-ing (*Wesung des Seyns*).

a) Echo

Echo names the way in which the thinking of *Contributions* first experiences be-ing's essential swaying in the transition from the first to the other beginning of Western history. The German word for "echo" in *Contributions* is *"Anklang."* In current German, *Anklang* denotes the initial moment in which a sound arises but has not yet fully unfolded. It carries the sense of silence and expectation, of withdrawal and intimation. "What" echoes (*klingt an*), the essential swaying of be-ing, is nothing but an occurrence that bears precisely these characteristics: withdrawal, silence, expectation, and intimation.

---

1. Heidegger is not consistent in the way he writes *"Seinsverlassenheit"* and *"Seinsvergessenheit."* Sometimes he writes them with a "y" (this is more often the case with *"Seynsvergessenheit"*), sometimes not. Although *"Seyn"* in distinction to *"Sein"* marks be-ing thought be-ing-historically in distinction to being thought metaphysically or transcendentally in relation to beings, the distinction between "y" and "i" is less crucial in these words (*Seinsvergessenheit* and *Seinsverlassenheit*). One could assume that Heidegger mostly writes *"Seinsverlassenheit"* because this word refers to beings (*Seiendes*) and their abandonment by being. On the other hand this abandonment indicates the way be-ing occurs, and thus it makes perfect sense also to write *"Seynsverlassenheit."*

At the end of metaphysics, be-ing is first experienced when its essential occurrence echoes in a withdrawal. Be-ing echoes "out of the abandonment of being through the compelling* distress (*nötigende Not*) of the forgottenness of be-ing" (C75; B107). In startled dismay and awe, thinking experiences the abandonment and forgottenness of be-ing as it finds itself struck by distress. This distress reveals that be-ing sways *as* withdrawal, i.e., being is not "something" that withdraws but an occurrence which has the characteristic of withdrawal. But be-ing does not only occur as withdrawal; if thinking remains attuned by startled dismay and awe and acknowledges the distress of be-ing, this distress becomes compelling; it calls for a response. In this compelling call we find the moment of expectation or intimation, i.e., an inceptual arising or emerging, which comes together with the experience of be-ing as withdrawal.

In echo, thinking is already set out into the time-space of decision that frames and articulates the whole jointure of *Contributions:* the decision over be-ing's historicality, i.e., whether being withdraws definitively or whether it occurs again inceptively. Thinking finds itself in this decision, compelled to take a stance in it. This compelling is what Heidegger addresses when he says: "The echo of be-ing wants to retrieve be-ing in its *full essential swaying* as enowning, by disclosing the abandonment of being" (C81; B116). In order to sway fully, be-ing needs to occur historically as an enowning event that permeates beings, and not anymore as one that only withdraws from beings. According to Heidegger, this withdrawal risks becoming so dominant that any possibility of be-ing's occurrence as enowning disappears. This would be the ultimate end of the history of be-ing.

b) Abandonment and Forgottenness of Being

As Heidegger points out, the abandonment of being and the forgottenness of being designate more originarily what Nietzsche recognized as *nihilism* (C80, 83; B115, 119). They name not only a personal experience but an epochal occurrence concerning Western history which Heidegger, like Nietzsche, finds rooted in ancient Greece and whose dominance unfolds in Christianity and is consolidated in modernity.[2] Thus, in *Contributions*, the abandonment of being carries a double sense: in a narrow sense, it indicates a clearly privative mode in which beings are abandoned by being; beings are deprived of their very essence (being) in what Heidegger conceives as the present era of machination. In a wider sense, the abandonment of being also indicates positively be-ing's occurrence; be-ing is experienced to sway essentially as withdrawal, yet a withdrawal through which beings may become manifest as such. "Be-ing *shelters and conceals itself* in the manifestness of beings" (C78; B111). The withdrawal of be-ing allows the appearing of things. When this occurrence of be-ing happens and is experienced originarily, trees, mountains, humans, animals, utensils, words, etc., appear as such in their *being*, i.e., in that they are and how they are. Thus, in the withdrawal of be-ing, beings are brought into their own, and be-ing occurs as enowning. Yet this withdrawal and enowning (this temporal event as which be-ing occurs) tends to conceal itself "behind" *what* it lets appear: beings. As a consequence, instead of being experienced in their temporal eventuation and passing away, beings are represented (*vorgestellt*) as constantly present substances with certain attributes. In this determination of beings, be-ing "refuses" (*versagt; verweigert*) its essence and beings remain abandoned by being.

Heidegger especially conceives this occurrence of be-ing's withdrawal into the manifestness of beings in relation to ancient Greek thought, which will be developed in more detail in the next joining of *Contributions*, "Playing Forth." He thinks the withdrawal of be-ing ("of" in the double sense that be-ing occurs *as withdrawal* and that this *withdrawal withdraws* from the manifestness of beings) as "the basic event of our history" (C78; B112). According to Heidegger, it is a history in which be-ing's withdrawal and with it the occurrence of the coming to be of beings conceals itself more and more until this essential occurring of be-ing is in danger ultimately of being covered up.

This happens when the abandonment of being is definitively consolidated in the *forgottenness of being* (C75; B107). The forgottenness of being

2. As his Nietzsche lecture courses testify, Heidegger finds in Nietzsche's philosophy the ultimate consolidation of the abandonment of being.

is rooted in the abandonment of being insofar as it is a consequence of the latter. It marks the consolidation of the abandonment insofar as the *"forgottenness of being* is not aware of itself; it presumes to be at home with 'beings' and with what is 'actual,' 'true' to 'life,' and certain of 'lived experience'" (C80; B114). Not aware of itself, the forgottenness of being is satisfied with the ways it represents and experiences beings, and this does not leave any room or sense of necessity for the question of be-ing itself as a temporal event which is totally outside the realm of representation and the calculability of beings. So it is that the forgottenness of being inaugurates what Heidegger calls "the epoch of total lack of questioning" (*das Zeitalter der völligen Fraglosigkeit*) (C75, 76; B108). The question of be-ing disappears in the domination of calculation and makeability; beings remain "dis-owned"* (*ent-eignet*) of (by) be-ing (C84; B120) and be-ing occurs as self-refusal (*Sich-verweigern; Sich-versagen*).

It is then, in the utmost "distress of distresslessness" (*Not der Notlosigkeit*), when nothing appears question-worthy (*fragwürdig*) anymore, that, in startled dismay and awe, this withdrawing character of be-ing may become manifest. But, certainly, in the moment thinking experiences the abandonment of being and the forgottenness of being *as such*, it shifts into an untimely situation, the transitory (*übergänglich*) situation which marks *Contributions*. Utmost abandonment and forgottenness are experienced and conceived in their epochal quality, and yet thinking is displaced with respect to this epochal manifestation into a more original realm of being. This more original realm is the time-space of decision over be-ing's historical eventuation, i.e., the decision whether be-ing will withdraw and remain definitively forgotten, or whether another beginning of the history of be-ing will inaugurate and determine a new epoch of Western history. It is here, in this dis-placement into a more original realm of being, that the essential swaying of be-ing echoes and shows itself to occur as withdrawal and refusal. It is here that thinking understands the abandonment of being as a historical occurrence which marks an epoch of Western history. In this dis-placement, thinking finds itself also compelled to let this abandonment of being become manifest so that the essential swaying of be-ing may echo epochally. *Contributions* attempts to prepare this by grounding being-t/here (*Da-sein*), i.e., the time-space of an inceptive occurring of be-ing which may unfold into another beginning of the history of be-ing.

Meanwhile, according to Heidegger, the abandonment of being and the forgottenness of being dominate the present epoch. In section 58 he reflects especially on three ways in which the abandonment of being becomes manifest. He calls these *symptoms* or *concealments of the abandonment of being*, concealments (*Verhüllungen*) that were prominent not only in the domination of National Socialism at the time Heidegger wrote these sections, but probably also today. The three concealments of the abandonment of being Heidegger stresses are *"calculation," "acceleration,"* and *"the outbreak of massiveness."* In calculation, beings are approached through guiding principles and rules. Calculation appears in the dominance of organization: everything is regulated through calculation; nothing escapes the possibility of calculation since any human comportment is always already guided by it. Acceleration permeates all comportment toward beings, too. We find it in "the mechanical increase of technical 'speeds'" and in "the mania for what is surprising, for what immediately sweeps [us] away and impresses [us]" (C84; B121). The outbreak of massiveness indicates the dominance of "what is common to the *many* and to *all*" (C84; B121f), which of course is facilitated through calculation and acceleration. All this, says Heidegger, spreads "in the semblance of an 'important' event" (C84; B122). Yet, according to Heidegger, calculation, acceleration, and the outbreak of massiveness are only symptoms of a more originary occurrence, the way be-ing occurs at the end of the first beginning of Western history. Here, be-ing occurs as machination (*Machenschaft*) and lived experience (*Erlebnis*).

c) Machination and Lived Experience

Heidegger stresses that machination is not a human comportment but the way be-ing occurs in the first beginning of Western history, i.e., in metaphysics. As is the case with the abandonment of being, machination can be understood in a wider or in a narrowed sense. In the wide sense, it indicates a relation to beings in the light of their makeability. Heidegger finds the roots of this relation in the way *techne* and *poiesis* determine the interpretation of *phusis* in ancient Greece.[3] But in ancient Greece, says Heidegger, machination does not yet fully come to light. Machination becomes more dominant in the Middle Ages through the Judeo-Christian notion of creation; all beings are *made* by God and thus become explainable according to the schema of cause and effect. This schema is further intensified in modern thinking in the increasing dominance of science and technology. But whereas in the Middle Ages beings were viewed as caused and created by God, in modernity they are seen as being caused (at least in their appearance) by subjectivity. Beings become objects (*Gegenstände*, things that stand over against the subject) of the human mind, and find their interpretation in relation to the human mind. As Kant teaches us, nature and objects as they appear to us are constituted by the categories of understanding, which are ultimately rooted in the unity of the transcendental ego. "We" "make" the world as it appears to us.

Machination, in the narrow sense, indicates that at the end of metaphysics be-ing tends to sway *only* as—and thus to conceal itself fully in—the makeability of beings. At this limit, the counterpart of machination, which belongs to it essentially, emerges. It is the way machination appears when it sways predominantly, the appearance under which machination hides itself so that its swaying becomes invisible, imperceptible: lived experience (*Erlebnis*). Lived experience appears under the dominance of subjectivity. We should note that subjectivity, as Heidegger understands it, does not indicate a character belonging to a human subject. Rather it means the dominance of thinking and representation (*Vorgestelltheit*) over the being of beings. (The concept "human subject" is another represented being like any other object.) In the domination of subjectivity, be-

3. We may recall at this point the Platonic concept of *idea* or *eidos* as that which guides *techne* and, thus, is thought in relation to *techne*: the form (*idea*) of a chair guides the carpenter in the know-how (*techne*) to make the chair. Heidegger considers the dominance of *techne* in the interpretation of *phusis* as an event that is rooted precisely in *phusis*, in be-ing. Thus, the overpowering of *techne* is an event necessitated by be-ing itself. See in this respect Heidegger's lecture course of summer 1935 *Introduction to Metaphysics*, trans. Richard Polt and Gregory Fried (New Haven, Conn.: Yale University Press, 2000). German edition: *Einführung in die Metaphysik*, ed. P. Jaeger (Klostermann: Frankfurt am Main, 1983 [GA 40]).

ings become objects *for* subjectivity and their being appears to dissolve more and more into the subjectivity which determines and produces them.[4] In section 63, Heidegger explains "lived experience" as follows: "To relate beings as that which is represented to *oneself* as the relational center and thus to draw them into 'life'"* (C90; B129). Beings acquire their being by coming to subjectivity; they get their sense through subjectivity and its "lived experience." Insofar as beings find their sense only in their relatedness to subjective life, they remain dis-enowned, they lose their being. What is most frightening in this occurrence is that the abandonment of being is masked by an occurrence which appears to be most alive. For Heidegger, this "life" engendered in lived experience suffocates any need to question be ing. Beings are not only calculable and producible—thus satisfying our need for security—but are also pleasurable and exciting—thus satisfying our need for discovery and novelty. What else should one look for?

d) The Gigantic

In the total abandonment of being, the occurrence of be-ing is turned into the possibility of its own disempowerment: what sways is not be-ing in its essential occurrence (*Wesen*) but be-ing in its un-essential occurrence* (*Unwesen*). This un-essential occurrence of be-ing in machination and lived experience is brought to completion also in the reign of the gigantic (*das Riesenhafte*). Here machination and lived experienced are completed insofar as they encounter no more boundaries. In the gigantic, beings are discovered through their boundless calculability and makeability. Any being is always already discovered as quantitatively calculable. Indeed, what beings are, their *quale*, is understood as quantity (C, section 70).

---

4. Heidegger discusses this process, for instance, in his Nietzsche lecture course of summer 1939 "Nietzsche's Doctrine of the Will to Power as Knowledge," in *Nietzsche*, Vol. III, ed. David Farrell Krell (San Francisco: HarperCollins, 1991). German edition: *Nietzsches Lehre vom Willen zur Macht als Erkenntnis*, ed. E. Hanser, Klostermann (Frankfurt am Main, 1989 [GA 47]). Beings are posited by subjectivity in a process of production (*Schaffen*) which includes the destruction and overcoming of former positings.

Again, this process is rooted for Heidegger in the first beginning, in ancient Greek thought, in the overpowering of *phusis* through *techne*. This process begins with the Greek experience of being as *phusis*, i.e., as an emerging of beings. But soon *techne*, the "know-how" to make things, determines the Greek approach to being so that being comes to be presented analogously to makeable beings. Consequently, being is determined as beingness (*Seiendheit*) and appears to be makeable and quantitatively calculable, like beings. And, as is the case with the abandonment of being and machination, at the end of metaphysics the gigantic tends to permeate the being of beings completely in the reign of technology. Representation (*Vor-stellen*) becomes "a *grasping* that reaches ahead, plans and arranges everything before everything is already conceived as particular and singular." This representing finds "no limit in the given"; it is "bound to *no given* and to no giveable as *limit*" (C94f; B136). If we conceive what is given as the horizon of objectivity or of the phenomena that show themselves, we may say that in the gigantic this horizon becomes totally enveloped in the presenting productivity of a subjectivity. Beings lose their own being to the productivity of subjectivity which finds no limits in what is given because what is given is given by itself in a motion of endless overpowerment.

In the thirties and forties, Heidegger develops his interpretations of the end of the first beginning, in terms of the completion of metaphysics in boundless subjectivity, primarily in his Nietzsche lecture courses. Later on, he develops his thought of machination in what he calls *"Gestell."* The Nietzsche lecture courses, as well as all his writings on technology after the thirties, develop against the background of the be-inghistorical thought of *Contributions* and, more specifically, of the "Echo" joining. Concerning Nietzsche, Heidegger reflects critically in several places on the position Nietzsche occupies in his be-ing-historical thinking.[5] In Heidegger's view, Nietzsche occupies the positions of one who

5. Martin Heidegger, *Was heisst Denken?* (Tübingen: Max Niemeyer Verlag, 1984), p. 21; "The Will to Power as Knowledge and as Metaphysics," in *Nietzsche*, Vol. III, pp. 156–157. German edition: *Nietzsches Lehre vom Willen zur Macht als Erkenntnis* (GA 47, p. 272).

completes metaphysics[6] and of one who is in a transition to another beginning. The latter occurs when Nietzsche's philosophy is taken as an essential *"Stoss,"* a push for a transformation of being which opens the space of the transition from the first to the other beginning, a space of decision over the destiny of Western history.

e) Modern Science

Heidegger concludes the "Echo" joining with several sections devoted to science. The consideration of modern science especially belongs to the "Echo" joining because science is essentially rooted in machination. Modern science co-decides the abandonment of being, but as Heidegger stresses, *"only insofar as* modern science claims to be one or even *the* decisive knowing"* (C98; B141). In that case it finds no need of a grounding of science since it knows itself and is certain about itself as the ground of all knowledge. Heidegger reflects especially on experimental exact science. Exact sciences have already pre-determined their subject matter as being accessible through quantitative measuring and calculation (C104; B150). Only as a consequence do these sciences need the experiment that serves to test regularities which from the outset regulate and direct the experiment quantitatively. All this is conditioned by a mathematical projection of nature.

6. In his lecture course of 1939 he interprets Nietzsche's will to power as the highest form of machination (GA 47, p. 324).

4. PLAYING-FORTH

The relation between the first and the other beginning, or, to be more precise, the in-between, the transition* (*Übergang*) between the first and the other beginning that first articulates the beginnings into the first and the other is the main concern of the second joining. This joining plays intimately into the first, transversing it, because, in the moment that thinking realizes the abandonment of being, it is already set out into this in-between of the first and the other beginning. Or, one could as well say, in being set out in the grounding attunement of startled dismay and awe, the in-between, the transition, first opens up. In the "Echo" joining, the abandonment of being is already conceived as a historical occurrence, and so is the compelling call to prepare the time-space for another beginning, a beginning in which the truth of be-ing occurs epochally as enowning. The preparation of this time-space arises in a deciding encounter (*Auseinandersetzung*) with the first beginning, especially with that which is inceptive in the first beginning. Thus, in the "Playing-Forth" joining, we find sections that thematize the transition from the first to the other beginning, and sections devoted to ancient Greek thought, as well as to the whole history of metaphysics derived from it. As Heidegger says in the first section of the "Playing-Forth" joining (section 81, C119; B169), to this joining belongs everything concerning the transition from the guiding question (*Leitfrage*) of metaphysics, where being is questioned analogously to beings, to the grounding question (*Grundfrage*)[1] of be-ing-historical thinking, where be-ing is questioned in its truth, as well as all of Heidegger's lecture courses about the history of philosophy.

---

1. Heidegger speaks of the "guiding question" and not of the "grounding question" of metaphysics because metaphysics is not able to question being in its occurrence as abysmal ground; in questioning being analogously to beings, metaphysics does not reach the "ground" of be-ing.

a) The Deciding Encounter of the First and the Other Beginning

The most difficult challenge of this section is *not* to understand the playing-forth of the first and the other beginning as a linear process departing in the past and reaching out to the future. Rather, this joining, like all joinings, occurs primarily in and as a decision that ultimately concerns the possibility of another beginning of history. In playing-forth, the first and the other beginning are first *"aus-einander-gesetzt"*; they are posited (*gesetzt*) in their decision (differentiation) (*aus-*) and encounter (*einander*). "Playing-forth," says Heidegger in section 82, "is a first 'bridging over'* into the transition,* a bridge that swings out to a shore [the beginnings] that must first be decided" (ibid.). To keep be-ing-historical thought free from all linearity is probably an impossible task since we are used to thinking in linear motions. But the reader may at least get a sense that a linear interpretation or view of history derives from this deciding encounter of the first and the other beginning, i.e., that linear thinking is rooted in it. For Heidegger, history (*Geschichte*) needs to be understood as an occurrence (*Geschehen*) of be-ing. "History" (*Historie*) understood as a linear sequence of observable "historical" (*historisch*) events arises in a representational way of thinking which has precisely lost the event-character of be-ing. In order to avoid as far as possible a linear presentation of history as we read *Contributions*, we may attempt to hold our thinking in the guiding attunement of reservedness and to hold on to the inceptive motion, to the first arising of a decision in which a differentiation into the first and the other, into past and future, is not yet fully articulated.

Since originarily the deciding encounter of the first and the other beginning is not a linear event, we must be careful how we originarily understand the words "beginning," "first," and "other." It is not clear, at the outset, if we are dealing with one or two beginnings, or if we should even make this differentiation. Interestingly, Heidegger never speaks of a "second beginning." On the contrary, in section 1 Heidegger says that the other beginning is named thus "because it must be the only other out of the relation *to the only one* and first beginning"*[2] (C4; B5). This suggests that

2. Italics added. Here the Emad-Maly translation is misleading in translating *"zu dem einzig einen und ersten Anfang"* as "to the one and only first beginning." The Emad-Maly translation suggests that there is one first beginning and not—as the German—that there is only one beginning.

there is one beginning, articulated into first and other. On the other hand, first and other clearly mark a differentiation, and what Heidegger writes never suggests that there is a transcendent beginning that is subsequently split into first and other. For representational thinking, the "relation" between the first and the other beginning necessarily remains an enigma; we represent to ourselves either one or two or three (the first, the other, and the transcendental) beginnings. In order to understand the "relation" between, or rather the in-between of the first and the other beginning, we need to attempt to think be-ing-historically, and this means inceptively; it is in inceptive thinking, in being dis-placed from presentational thinking in the acknowledgment of being's withdrawal, that the difference of presentational thinking and a thinking in the acknowledgment of being's withdrawal first emerges. This difference differentiates the first and the other beginning in some respect. The one beginning we attempt to think is not something out there, rather, it occurs *as* we think, and as we think inceptively, a differentiation occurs. This differentiation is further articulated in the interpretations of philosophers of our tradition *as* we read their texts in the light of inceptive thinking, of a thinking which occurs in the attuning range and thoughtful acknowledgment of being's withdrawal and, thus, in the attunement to another to our tradition.

Yet the other to our metaphysical tradition does not arise from some place alien to that tradition; it arises in it, from a more originary, inceptive understanding of it. The other arises out of the first, and the first appears as first only in the light of the other. The other beginning arises in a deciding encounter with the history of philosophy, and the first beginning of this history appears as such only in the intimation of another beginning of history. The first and the other beginning arise for thinking in their playing-forth.

Still the question remains: Why should Heidegger speak of a "first" beginning? It is "known" that, for Heidegger, the first beginning designates the beginning of the Western history of being, which begins in ancient Greek thought and which ends with Nietzsche, an ending which continues even now. But this ending also belongs to the beginning. We may therefore differentiate between a narrow and a wider sense of the first beginning. In a narrow sense, "first beginning" indicates the arising of metaphysics as Heidegger elaborates it in his reading of the Presocratics, Plato, and Aristotle. In a wider sense it encompasses the entire history of metaphysics up to our time. In this account of the first beginning, we interpret "first" in relation to a linear history. But, as noted earlier, this linear interpretation is not originary. There must be, then, another sense of "first," a sense of the first arising in relation to the other. Indeed, Heidegger develops the thought of the other beginning through a more originary interpretation of the first beginning. Thus, the other can only occur through the first.

Even though the other beginning emerges out of a more originary interpretation of the first, Heidegger stresses that "other" does not mean "over against," as if the other beginning took the opposite direction to the first (which would reinscribe it into the first). Rather, the other beginning is called "other" because "*as the other* it stands outside an opposition* (*Gegen*) and outside immediate comparability"³ (C131; B187). This other beginning plays into the be-ing-historical thinking of *Contributions* in a twofold way. On the one hand, we hear that playing-forth is the "preparation for the other beginning" (C119; B169). Be-ing-historical thinking is meant to prepare the other beginning, which implies that this other beginning in some sense is "not yet." In the other beginning, the truth of be-ing would occur as en-owning, would permeate all beings, and thus would initiate another epoch of Western history. On the other hand, in the moment this thinking is set out into the more originary realm of the truth of be-ing, in this time-space of transition that was called earlier "an untimely situation," it has overcome the first beginning (C120; B171, section 85). In this transition, says Heidegger in section 1, the other beginning is only intimated (as an occurrence that historically initiates another epoch of the history of be-ing) and yet is already decided (in thinking) (C3; B4). In section 89 he writes:

> The transition to the other beginning is decided and yet we do not know where we are going, when the truth of be-ing becomes something true

3. Compare also the following passage of section 91: "Leaping into the other beginning is returning into the first beginning, and vice versa. But returning into the first beginning (the 'retrieval' (*Wiederholung*)) is not displacement into what has passed, as if this could be

and from where the history as the history of be-ing takes its steepest and shortest path.* (C124; B177)

After this more formal explanation of the first and the other beginning, we will now consider more closely what occurs in the beginning/s. And since the other beginning arises in the more original positing of the first, we may consider the first beginning first.

b) The More Original Positing of the First Beginning

Crucial for the first beginning is its beginning and its end. We have already noted how the end is experienced and conceived in the "Echo" joining. As far as its inceptive beginning is concerned, it occurs in ancient Greek philosophy. Of course, Heidegger's reading of the Greeks does not aim at interpreting the Greeks for their own sake or as they would have interpreted themselves. Rather, Heidegger's interpretation of the Greeks occurs in the deciding encounter (*Auseinandersetzung*) with the Greeks, i.e., in an encounter in which the Greeks are already displaced (*versetzt*) in the light of another thought.

The decisive moments marking the first beginning are the Greek experience of the truth of be-ing in the notions of *phusis* and *aletheia*, the overpowering (*Übermächtigung*) of *phusis* through *techne*, the breakdown (*Einsturz*) of *aletheia*, and, concurrently, the differentiation of being and thinking (of *phusis* and *logos*) which marks presentational (*vorstellungshaftes*) thinking. According to Heidegger, Greek thinking originates in an original experience of the truth of be-ing, i.e., not only of the presencing belonging to it, but also of its occurring as withdrawal. This is indicated, for Heidegger, in the Greek word for truth: *a-letheia*, which he translates as "un-concealment," an unconcealment which presupposes an experience of concealment. Heidegger believes that even if the Greeks did experience concealment they were not able to conceive this

---

made 'actual' again in the usual sense. Returning into the first beginning is rather and precisely distancing from it, is taking up that distant-positioning which is necessary in order to experience what began in it and as that beginning" (C130; B185).

concealment belonging to the truth of be-ing as such. However, the fact that they were not able to think this original event is, according to Heidegger, not a failure of their thinking, but a necessity rooted in how the truth of be-ing occurs in the first beginning. As Heidegger understands it, in his interpretation of the Presocratics as well as of the chorus song of Sophocles' *Antigone*, the overpowering emerging swaying of be-ing as *phusis* forces *logos* to find a stand in the midst of it by finding a stand over against what appears in it[4] (C133; B190). In this process, thinking is forced to differentiate itself from the occurrence of be-ing out of which it emerges and to find a stand in a questioning of *what* appears in the event of be-ing. Consequently, being is questioned, in reference to the beings which appear, in terms of its (being's) presence and permanence (beingness). The question of being turns into the *guiding question* (*Leitfrage*) of metaphysics about the beingness of beings. Since it is the overpowering occurrence of be-ing as *phusis* (emerging swaying) that forces this differentiation of being and thinking, in which being comes to be questioned and represented as the being of beings, Heidegger can say that be-ing withdraws *itself* "behind" the appearance of beings.

In relation to the "Echo" joining, we already saw that in Heidegger's reading of the history of philosophy, the withdrawal of be-ing unfolds as a history of a more and more complete abandonment of being until it reaches a limit where the forgottenness of being compels thinking so that thinking is set out into the original sway of being as withdrawal. This marks the moment of transition from the guiding question (being as beingness) to the *grounding question* of the truth of be-ing.

By asking the grounding question, thinking rethinks and thus reappropriates the hidden ground of the first beginning, that is, the truth of be-ing which occurs as unconcealing-concealment and out of which things come to presence. Consequently, the history of the first beginning (of metaphysics) becomes ambiguous (*zweideutig*) (C120; B171, section 85). On

---

4. See in this context Heidegger's lecture course of summer 1935 *Introduction to Metaphysics*. In German: *Einführung in die Metaphysik* (GA40). For a more detailed discussion of *phusis* in this context, see Susan Schoenbohm, "Heidegger's Interpretation of Phusis," in *A Companion to Heidegger's Introduction to Metaphysics*, ed. Richard Polt and Gregory Fried (New Haven, Conn.: Yale University Press, 2001), Chapter 8 (pp. 143–160).

the one hand, metaphysics appears on the surface, so to speak, as a questioning of being as beingness, as permanent presence in the forgetfulness of being's withdrawal. On the other hand, metaphysics appears in the light of its hidden and more originary history as the history of the truth of be-ing. This offers a new way of interpreting metaphysics with respect to what is hidden in it and makes it possible, i.e., with respect to its concealed beginning.

c) The Other Beginning

We have seen that, conceived as the beginning of a new epoch of Western history, the other beginning remains concealed. But, in understanding more originarily the first beginning, thinking finds the other beginning to be already intimated and decided for thinking. It is in the light of the more original understanding of the first beginning that the other, in its possibility,[5] begins. In section 91 Heidegger writes:

> In the *other beginning* truth is recognized and grounded as the truth of be-ing and be-ing is recognized and grounded as be-ing of truth, i.e., as *enowning which is in itself a turning event** [*ein in sich kehriges Ereignis*], to which belongs the inner issuance [*Ausfall*] of the cleft* [*Zerklüftung*] and thus the abyss*. (C130; B185)

Truth which is grounded in the other beginning is truth that remained ungrounded in the first beginning, i.e., truth as an occurrence of discovering (letting appear) *and* withdrawal, truth as unconcealing concealment. This truth remained ungrounded in the first beginning since truth (as unconcealment) was taken to be a characteristic of beings as such. It remained a characteristic of beings especially because the concealment belonging to the truth of be-ing could not be conceived as such. Consequently, the first task for inceptive thinking in the transition from the first to the other beginning is to remain exposed to the experience of this con-

---

5. Note that in this context "possibility" (*Möglichkeit*) is not opposed to an actuality but means capacity (*Vermögen*).

cealment and thus to let it occur. And inceptive thinking lets the concealment occur by saying inceptively about this concealment. This letting occur and bringing to language is, in part, what Heidegger calls the grounding of being-t/here. The task of grounding more originarily the truth of be-ing in being-t/here is, according to *Contributions*, a necessity which is rooted in the compelling distress which arises when thinking acknowledges and experiences the danger of the utmost withdrawal of being in the dominance of machination and lived experience. The grounding of the truth of be-ing in being-t/here is what Heidegger *attempts* to accomplish in *Contributions*. This grounding would not yet mark the epochal beginning of the other beginning but would "only" prepare the time-space for this event. It is only in this event that the truth of be-ing would sway as enowning in such a way that it enowns and therefore shines through beings, permeating all realms of human comportment.

The playing-forth of the first and the other beginning is not only essential for the grounding of the truth of be-ing in being t/here; it is in itself a grounding of this truth. As Heidegger notes in section 82, the historical meditation (*geschichtliche Besinnung*) that occurs in playing-forth already requires the leap into the truth of be-ing which, in turn, occurs as a grounding of this truth. The inceptive thinking of playing-forth requires that thinking be set out into the more originary realm of the history of being, the realm in which *Contributions* moves not only "after" the first two joinings, but in all six joinings.

5. LEAP

The "Playing-Forth" joining explores the domain of the history of be-ing with respect to the first and the other beginning, which are de-cided in it. The "Leap" joining explores this domain with respect to the way it sways, i.e., as an abysmal occurrence in which being-t/here, humans, and gods are enowned.

As noted already above, in the opening section of this joining the leap is called "the most daring move in the proceeding of* inceptual thinking" since "it abandons and throws aside everything familiar, expecting nothing from beings immediately" (C161; B227). This has nothing to do with the courageous leap of a human subject that throws itself into nothingness. According to Heidegger, it is an occurrence necessitated by the acknowledgment of the utmost abandonment of being. Humans are not the agents of this occurrence; instead, they find their transformed being first *in* this occurrence. They find their being to be fundamentally exposed and open to the abysmal truth of be-ing out of which it arises, i.e., it finds itself enowned. So it is that the leap is a risk. It abandons the usual representational relation to things which grants us some sense of familiarity, security, and "groundedness" as we plan and live our daily lives. However, if in the leap thinking lets go of everything familiar and leaps into no-thing, "something" opens up in the leap which grants thinking a different kind of dwelling. What opens up is the historical *occurrence* of be-ing as enowning withdrawal. "The leap is the risk* (*das Wagnis*) of an initial foray into the domain of the history of being* (*Seinsgeschichte*)," says Heidegger, and it "leaps into* [*erspringt*] belongingness to be-ing in its full essential swaying as enowning" (ibid.). As thinking lets go of everything familiar, in the leap it finds itself enowned, brought to be in an event without (metaphysical) "ground." Thinking finds itself enowned in being-t/here, together with gods, an earth, a world, and other beings.

This leads to three main themes that are unfolded in the leap: a) the truth of be-ing as enowning, b) the relation between enowning and withdrawal ("being and nothingness"), and c) what is enowned in enowning: being-t/here, gods, and humans.[1]

a) The Inceptive Opening of the Truth of Be-ing as Enowning

The leap is attuned by awe, by a silent hesitating reservedness in which thinking abides in the opening of be-ing's withdrawal. This opening of the truth of be-ing in being-t/here does not occur after the leap, nor does it exist before the leap; it opens *as* the leap occurs. The reader of *Contributions* should recall, especially in this context, that what Heidegger thinks and attempts to say in this book is what opens up inceptively *as* he thinks it. Accordingly, it does not make any sense to speak of a "be-ing" which is there before its opening for thinking. Being is disclosed in thinking both as an abysmal and as an enowning event, and thinking finds itself in this event in what Heidegger calls "a leap of thinking." In this leap, thinking experiences that it does nothing but respond to a "throw" or "call" of be-ing which at the same time becomes manifest as such only in this response.[2]

In the leap, thinking finds itself being t/here in an abysmal opening of a historical (i.e., determined) time-space. This being-t/here is itself experienced in a rising motion out of be-ing's withdrawal as being enowned, as being given to be, brought to its "own." "Be-ing holds sway as *enowning the grounding of the t/here [Da]*, put briefly: as *enowning.*" (C174; B247). So be-ing occurs as *enowning of* the t/here, i.e., the clearing of its truth (its occurrence in unconcealing/concealment), but, in turn, be-ing only opens up as *enowning through* this clearing of being-t/here. This is why Heidegger speaks of the turning (*Kehre*) in which the truth of be-ing as enowning occurs. The t/here is enowned, but at the same time the enowning of the grounding of the t/here first clears the self-concealment* (*Sichverbergen*), and, with this self-concealment, the enowning. Enown-

---

1. How earth, world, and other beings come into play is discussed in the next joining, "Grounding."
2. See section 122.

ing occurs as the turning "in-between" self-concealing-enownment and grounding of the t/here.[3]

The grounding of the t/here, Heidegger says, is "what is more originary of *being-t/here* [*Da-sein*]" (ibid.), i.e., the opening (the t/here) is more originary than the being (abiding) of humans in the t/here. But, if be-ing is to hold sway in being-t/here, if it is to find a historical timespace in which it may occur as enowning, according to Heidegger, it needs humans. As noted earlier,[4] in *Contributions* Heidegger thinks humans not primarily as entities but rather in their being and in determinations that arise out of their *being* the t/here. By abiding in the clearing of the withdrawal of be-ing, humans *are* the t/here, they make possible the being of the t/here in being-t/here. And this, in turn, first brings humans to their essential determination. This is why Heidegger says in section 133, "Be-ing needs humans* in order to hold sway; and humans* belong to be-ing so that they can accomplish their utmost destiny as being-t/here* [*Da-sein*]" (C177; B251). Out of be-ing's need, which arises out of being's self-withdrawal, humans are enowned to *be* the t/here, and thus to hold open the disclosed site of the truth of be-ing. At the same time, in belonging to that site, humans allow be-ing to occur as they become essentially who they are. Again, enowning shows itself to sway as a turning in-between be-ing as enowning and being-t/here in human's belonging to it (ibid.).

At this point it is essential *not* to imagine a "be-ing" (beingness) on one side and a being-t/here or humans on the other side. Unfortunately, Heidegger's talk in his works of a "relation" between being and humans has caused many Heidegger interpreters to understand them as somehow separated or in opposition. But, as Heidegger notes in section 135, "the relation of Da-sein *to* be-ing belongs in the essential swaying of be-ing itself" (C179; B254). Da-sein, being-t/here, is the clearing *of* be-ing. It is the clearing *of* be-ing both in the sense that be-ing is cleared in being-t/here and in the sense that (in turn) the clearing arises out of being and thus belongs to be-ing.

---

3. See also sections 140 and 141.
4. Chapter 2, a) "*Contribution's* 'Grand Fugue.'"

b) Humans and Gods

The turning of enowning does not exhaust itself in the turning between the truth of be-ing and being-t/here and humans. There is another essential constituent of this turning that we need to consider, the gods. We consider them only now not because they are less important for Heidegger, but because they reach out from the most concealed and inceptive moment of enowning.

In the leap, the clearing of the truth of be-ing opens as being-t/here in the turning of enowning. Heidegger formulates this clearing with respect to its most concealed, as well as inceptive, character, as *cleft* (*Zerklüftung*). The word "cleft" carries the sense of a fissure in a mountain, a fissure without bottom, which cannot be closed and which divides the two "sides" of the fissure. Heidegger conceives this cleft in relation to the de-cision of gods and humans, and to the "nothingness" permeating it. We will see that gods and nothingness are intimately related.

In section 157, Heidegger writes, "In one direction the cleft* has its primary and broadest bearing in god's needing; and in the other direction, in humans' belongingness (to be-ing)" (C197; B279). The need of humans, of which Heidegger speaks in section 133, unfolds in *Contributions* not solely as a need belonging to be-ing, but as a need of the gods. In the withdrawal of be-ing which compels humans, the needing of the gods resonates. "'Gods' need be-ing in order through be-ing—which does not belong to gods—nevertheless to belong to themselves," says Heidegger in section 259 of *Contributions*. (C309; B438).

In order to understand why in be-ing-historical thinking the distress which compels this thinking into a more originary realm of the truth of be-ing unfolds as the need of the gods, we should take into account Heidegger's encounter with Hölderlin. It is Hölderlin who in his poems speaks of the flight of the gods, of their withdrawal, and who, at the same time, speaks of the hope of the return of the godly. Heidegger's reading of Hölderlin's poetry is essential for the be-ing-historical thinking of *Contributions* since, as Heidegger says also in his lecture course for the winter of 1934–35,[5] it is in poetry that the hints of the gods are revealed first.

---

5. Martin Heidegger, *Hölderlins Hymne "Germanien" und "Der Rhein"* (WS 34/35), ed. S. Ziegler (Klostermann: Frankfurt am Main, 1989; second edition GA 39), p. 32.

The question of the godly will be discussed in more detail in the sixth joining, "The Last God."[6] For now, it is important to see that the gods are considered by Heidegger, in relation to Hölderlin's poetry, out of their withdrawal, out of their not-being. This means that for being-historical thinking, gods are not first beings that then would manifest their need. They are first "perceived" out of their need precisely in their not being; they need the enownment of being-t/here in order to become manifest. Being-t/here, in turn, discloses only if humans respond to the need of the gods. Again, this does not mean that the need of the gods exists prior to the enownment of being-t/here. Their need is experienced only *as* thinking is set out into the more originary realm of the truth of be-ing as withdrawal and abides in this abysmal opening. The need of the gods and the response of humans occur at once in enowning. "En-owning owns god over [*übereignet*] to humans* in that it owns humans* to [*zueignet*] god" (C197; B280). Enowning owns the gods over to humans in the gods' need, and owns humans to the gods in humans' response to the need of the gods. Thus, humans are enowned in their being (in being-t/here) in relation to gods. Again, enowning occurs as *turning*. The turning in-between the truth of be-ing and being-t/here now unfolds as the turning that enowns and brings to their encounter gods and humans.

c) The Cleft: Be-ing and Nothingness

As indicated above, there is a close connection between the gods and "nothingness." Some indication of this connection lies in the fact that gods are not thought of as beings or entities that are; on the contrary, they lack being and need being. They sway in this lack, and this points to the swaying of be-ing as withdrawal and refusal.

For be-ing-historical thinking, the swaying of be-ing as refusal discloses itself inceptively in the cleft of be-ing. Refusal was explicated ear-

6. This joining will also discuss the relation between the plurality of the gods and the singularity of the "last god." For now they are treated without distinction with respect to their number.

lier (see "Echo") as the withdrawal aspect of be-ing's occurrence which thinking experiences in acknowledging the abandonment and forgottenness of being, i.e., when it experiences the utmost withdrawal of be-ing. It is then, as the withdrawal reaches its limit (the possibility of the impossibility), that thinking is compelled by the need of be-ing to "leap" into the be-ing's abysmal truth. Here thinking experiences be-ing's swaying as refusal in its abysmal and most inceptive opening in its cleft. In section 127 Heidegger says:

> The cleft* is the unfolding of the intimacy [*Innigkeit*][7] of be-ing itself, which remains in itself [*in sich bleibende*] in so far as we 'experience' it as refusal, a refusal that is encompassing [*Umweigerung*].* (C172; B244)

Be-ing is experienced as refusal when it remains in itself, i.e., when it does not sway as enowning in what Heidegger conceives as the present era of abandonment of being. And yet, refusal is not a mere negation of enowning but bears its possibility in terms of its necessity.[8] This is why Heidegger conceives this unfolding but at the same time self-enclosing character of the cleft of be-ing in relation to the *modalities*, even though he insists that the modalities are of no use in understanding the occurring of be-ing as cleft.

The modalities in metaphysics are reality, possibility, and necessity, and are derived from the questioning of beings or beingness. Accordingly, strictly speaking, they cannot be used to understand the occurrence of be-ing as cleft. And yet there is a relation between the modalities and the cleft since the cleft points to their original unity. *"One essential cleft is being in bending back* (capability, but not according to possibility, which up to now has always been thought in terms of beings as extant)" (C198; B281). Here, Heidegger regards the staying in itself of be-ing, its refusal, as capacity. This concept, "capacity" (*Vermögen*), does not stand in opposition

---

7. With respect to his Hölderlin lecture course of 1934–35 we can understand intimacy (*Innigkeit*) as an original unity of opposites, which in this case means that the cleaving apart remains united as well as separates while be-ing stays in itself. See GA 39, p. 117, and chapter three of the second part of the lecture course.
8. This is why "refusal" has a double meaning as explained in the following joining "Grounding," section a) "Being-t/here."

to reality and necessity, since the bending back, which is the aspect of withdrawal or refusal of being, occurs in and is necessary for the unfolding of be-ing. Refusal and opening of the cleft of be-ing occur together; they are one occurrence. The abysmal origin of the cleft ("of" in the two-fold sense), a cleft which de-cides gods and humans as they are brought into their own, remains in a reserve, withdraws as the cleft opens. It is not an unreachable ground which keeps the "mere possibility" of future histories of be-ing. Instead the bending back of the cleft is understood as ripeness* (*Reife*); ripeness is not *yet* a gift* or dissemination* (*Verschenkung*), but it *is* in the not yet; it is "pregnant with the originary 'not'" (C189; B268).

This sense of originating capacity that *is* a "not" appears earlier in *Being and Time* in which Heidegger thinks possibility (as capacity) out of the horizonal temporality of being, out of which Dasein temporalizes itself and beings are disclosed. We have seen in the first part of this study how the utmost possibility of being of Dasein is disclosed out of this temporalizing horizon in being-towards-death as the possibility of not-being. It is out of this possibility of not being that Dasein temporalizes itself and that being as such is disclosed. Heidegger also explores this connection between being-towards-death, disclosure, possibility (capacity), and nothingness in section 160 of *Contributions*, where he says that

> being-towards-death, unfolded as essential determination of the truth of Da-sein,[9] shelters within itself two fundamental determinations of the cleft* and is their, mostly unrecognized, mirroring in the t/here [*Da*]: *On the one hand* what is sheltered here is the essential belongingness of the not to being as such[. . .]. *On the other hand* being-towards-death shelters the unfathomable and essential richness of '*necessity*,' again as the one cleft of being itself [. . .]. (C198f; B282)

The cleft of be-ing opens in the leap as the abysmal occurrence of the truth of be-ing in its most inceptive swaying. This means that the leap is in itself grounding, in the sense that it first opens a historical time-space

---

9. This means that Da-sein, as Heidegger conceives it in *Contributions*, does not exhaust itself in being-towards-death but encloses it. See section 163, C200; B285.

of the truth of be-ing. The next joining, "Grounding," explores further that same realm of the history of be-ing into which thinking is set out in the acknowledgment of the abandonment and forgottenness of being and in the playing-forth of the first and the other beginning, this realm out of which be-ing-historical thinking finds itself enowned in the leap.

6. GROUNDING

We looked earlier at the double meaning of grounding which mirrors the turning of the truth of be-ing as which enowning occurs.[1] Since it is also essential in order to understand the way in which the "Grounding" joining moves, we should recall it to mind.[2] The first meaning of "grounding" refers to the truth of be-ing: the *truth* of be-ing, i.e., be-ing's unconcealing-concealment, occurs as grounding and so is called "ground." In the "Grounding" joining, Heidegger will further distinguish three other senses of this first meaning of ground: it occurs as *abyss (Abgrund)*, as *primordial ground (Urgrund)*, and as *unessential ground (Ungrund)*. These determinations all arise out of the way in which the truth of be-ing is experienced in the leap of thinking into the essential swaying of be-ing as self-refusal. If thinking remains attuned to reservedness in which this refusal of be-ing resonates and thus can be acknowledged, the truth of be-ing first opens as abyss. Out of this abyss, thinking also finds itself enowned and, thus, finds that the truth of be-ing occurs as enowning. As enowning, the truth of be-ing sways essentially as primordial ground. But, by being set out into this more original realm of the history of be-ing, thinking also acknowledges that for most people in the present era of machination and lived experience, the truth of be-ing never is experienced as such but remains covered, hidden. When the truth of be-ing remains hidden in its occurrence as abyss and in its occurrence as enowning, be-ing refuses its essential occurrence and, therefore, sways as unessential ground. So much for a preliminary exposition of the first meaning of grounding where it is viewed with respect to the truth of be-ing and its swaying as withdrawal (refusal) and enownment.

1. Chapter 2 a). Heidegger explicates the double meaning of grounding in section 187 of *Contributions*.
2. Note that this is only a preliminary exposition of the double meaning of "grounding." How this grounding occurs will be developed in more detail throughout this chapter.

The second sense of grounding is "projecting-grounding"* (*Er-grün-den*). Here, the same occurrence of grounding is explored with respect to how the truth of be-ing is let sway (*wesen lassen*) in being-t/here and how something is "built on" or "brought to" this original ground. This occurs through humans' abiding in Da-sein (being-t/here), which holds open and lets sway the t/here of the truth of be-ing by what Heidegger calls the "sheltering" (*Bergung*) of the truth of be-ing into beings. This occurs, for instance, in saying, painting, or sculpting, where truth is "sheltered" in words or works of art. We should recall, once again, that, of course, humans do not "do this" as independent subjects, but rather find themselves enowned in this very occurrence; they find themselves exposed to and given to be who they are by the truth of be-ing as it is held open (in its disclosure) in *being*-t/here through the sheltering of the truth of be-ing (the "t/here") in beings. The two senses of projecting-grounding, letting sway and building, reappear throughout Heidegger's work as two fundamental modes of sheltering the truth of be-ing.[3]

The "Grounding" joining is divided into five parts: a) "Da-sein and Projecting Being Open," b) "Da-sein," c) "The Essential Sway of Truth," d) "Time-Space as Abyss," e) "The Swaying of Truth as Sheltering." The first two parts thematize grounding in the sense of projecting-grounding. Here, Heidegger reflects on being-t/here (Da-sein) and the relation between humans and being-t/here. In the third and fourth parts, Heidegger meditates on the originary sense of grounding. Here we come to the heart of *Contributions*, to its most concealed core, where the *truth* of be-ing is unfolded as abyss and primordial ground (enowning)

The sequence of these first five parts mirrors the path of be-ing-historical thinking in the transition from the first to the other beginning of the history of be-ing in that it moves from a more original understanding of human *being* to the truth of be-ing. Coming from metaphysics, more specifically, from the metaphysics of subjectivity, the leap into the truth of be-ing requires above all a transformation of human being away from its

---

3. In "The Origin of the Work of Art," they are called "preserving" and "creating" (*Schaffen und Bewahren*) (in Martin Heidegger, *Basic Writings*, trans. David F. Krell [San Francisco; Harper San Francisco, 1992]); in "Building, Dwelling, Thinking" they are called "caring for" and "erecting" (*Pflegen und Errichten*) (in Heidegger, *Basic Writings*).

determination as subject (which Heidegger begins in *Being and Time*) and toward its understanding out of the historical swaying of the truth of be-ing. The last part of the "Grounding" joining is devoted to the question of sheltering the truth of be-ing in beings out of the original occurrence of the truth of be-ing, thereby bringing together the two aspects of grounding.

The following sections mostly retrace the line of thought into which the sections of the "Grounding" joining are arranged. However, they begin with an unfolding of being-t/here as the point of turning of enowning.[4] Then comes a thematization of how humans and thinking are enowned in the turning of enowning, to be followed by a discussion of the swaying of the truth of be-ing as abyss, i.e., as time-space, and as enowning. Finally, we will look at the sheltering of the truth of be-ing, not only with respect to what Heidegger says in *Contributions*, but also with respect to how he unfolds this question in "The Origin of the Work of Art," a text which is an essential supplement to the question of sheltering in *Contributions*.

a) Being-T/here

The hyphenation of *Da-sein* in *Contributions* marks a shift of the mean-ing of the word with respect to *Being and Time*. It no longer marks prima-rily human being, but the historical disclosure of the truth of being, the "turning point in the turning of enowning" (C219; B311), the "in-between" of humans and gods. The hyphen draws the attention of the reader to what resonates literally in this word: the *"Da-"* which designates the opening, the *t/here* of the truth of being, and the *"-sein"* which refers to the "abiding in," the *being* of humans *in* this opening, a being out of which they first find their own essence (*Wesen*). In order to distinguish the Da-sein of *Contributions* from the Dasein of *Being and Time* (to which it

---

4. I skip the reflections on "understanding of being" (*Seinsverständnis*) since they belong to the context of *Being and Time*. But I would like to remind the reader that Heidegger rethinks the *"understanding of being"* in being-historical terms as the *projection* (projecting-ground-ing) of the t/here that is itself "thrown," or—said being-historically—enowned by the truth of be-ing.

remains intimately related) and, above all, in order to avoid an understanding of Da-sein as some kind of being (*Seiendes*), it is always translated as "being-t/here."[5] The reader is invited to hear in "being-t/here" not primarily the being-t/here of humans but the "indefinite" being-t/here which discloses when we are unsettled in our everyday involvement with things and experience an inceptive opening of being, together with a sense of its passing quality.

To this, we need to add the be-ing-historical dimension this word carries. Being-t/here opens in the distress of the abandonment of being in which being occurs as self-refusal and, at the same time, remains concealed as this refusal in machination and lived experience. Being-t/here opens be-ing's epochal swaying as self-refusal. Consequently, being-t/here is the clearing of the self-concealment in which be-ing occurs at the end of metaphysics. Yet being-t/here discloses this occurrence of be-ing's self-refusal as such as it opens be-ing's inceptual occurrence in relation to the first and the other beginning. Heidegger finds that being-t/here discloses the *truth* of being (the unconcealment of be-ing's self-concealment) which is already the ground of the Greek experience and understanding of be-ing as *phusis*, even if the Greeks were not able to think that ground. Thus, in section 173 he writes, "Being-t/here is the very own self-grounding ground of *aletheia* of *phusis*, it is the essential swaying of that openness which first opens* [*eröffnet*] the self-concealing* [*Sichverbergen*] (the essential sway of be-ing) and which is thus the truth of be-ing itself" (C209; B296). To think this truth of be-ing as such as it discloses in being-t/here at the end of the first beginning opens at the same time the possibility of the other beginning of Western history.

Being-t/here does not encompass the truth of be-ing (the opening of its self-concealing) but is its clearing, a clearing which, in turn, arises out of (is enowned in) this self-concealing. It is out of this clearing that humans and gods are enowned. In section 190, Heidegger notes that

> Being-t/here is the occurrence of the opening cleft* [*Erklüftung*] of the turning-midpoint of the turning in enowning. Opening cleft* is en-ownment, above

---

5. "T/here" is used to render the double meaning of "here" and "there" that the German "da" has. Emad and Maly keep the German word sometimes untranslated (see "Foreword" to *Contributions*, xxxiv, xxxv).

all and primarily* [zuvor] the opening cleft from which [occur] *historical humans* and the essential swaying of being, nearing and distancing of gods.* (C218; B311)

The characteristics of the cleft discussed in the "Leap" joining, namely, the refusal that permeates it and its bearing to humans on one side and to gods on the other, are characteristics of the way the truth of be-ing sways in being-/there, i.e., they are characteristics of being-t/here. We saw in the first part of the present book[6] how the self-refusal or withdrawal of be-ing is mirrored in Heidegger's discussion of being-away [*Weg-sein*]. But, where the "refusal" indicates the swaying of the truth of be-ing, being-away indicates "what" is enowned in this occurring of the truth (being-t/here) and, in being enowned, keeps open—or conceals—the clearing of the truth of be-ing.

Just as there are two senses of *refusal* (*Versagung*) at play in *Contributions*, there are also two senses of *being-away*. In a more originary and larger sense, "refusal" indicates the way be-ing sways inceptively.[7] Correspondingly, being-away in the more originary sense means "the totally other to the t/here [*Da*], totally concealed from us, but *in this* concealedness* belonging essentially to the t/here [*Da*] and needing to be sustained along with the inabiding of being-*t/here*" (C228; B324). This originary sense of being-away is at play in death.[8] Yet being-away and refusal have also a secondary, more restricted sense. Refusal in this narrow sense indicates that in machination and lived experience, be-ing refuses its essential swaying and does not occur as enowning. Correspondingly, being-away in its narrow sense would be a synonym for forgottenness of being, or, as Heidegger says, the more original sense of inauthenticity (*Uneigentlichkeit*) (C213; B301f).

Even though being-t/here is the clearing out of which humans *and* gods emerge in their encounter, in the sections on Da-sein in the "Grounding" joining, Heidegger thematizes more the relation between being-t/here and humans. But, as we will see with reference to the last

---

6. Chapter 2, b).
7. See the previous joining, "Leap" c) The Cleft: Being and Nothingness.
8. See Chapter 2, b).

part of *Contributions* entitled "Be-ing," being-t/here and the truth of be-ing as enowning can be unfolded as well "from the side" of the gods.[9] For now let us stay with the sections under the title "Grounding" and see how humans find their selfhood out of being-t/here.

b) Being-T/here—Selfhood—Humans

In section 194, Heidegger says that in order to be them*selves,* humans need to be set out (*ver-rückt*) and thus grounded into being-t/here (C223; B317). This "grounding" occurs when humans remain attuned by reservedness and sustain in their "*being the* t/here" above all the withdrawal in which be-ing occurs. Humans find themselves exposed to this withdrawal, which is mirrored in their own death. Thus, the "self" Heidegger is thinking here is the authentic self which he also thinks in *Being and Time,* the self to which human beings come back only in resolute being-towards-death. This "self" first discloses the ownmost being of humans. Further, we will see that this self, which has nothing in common with a self-enclosed subject, occurs in the belongingness to the truth of being, a truth that is abysmal. It is therefore a self that is fundamentally open.

The coming to themselves of humans is grounded in what Heidegger calls "selfhood" (*Selbstheit*). This selfhood is prior to any "I," "you," and "we." Also it does not refer merely to a human "self." Rather, Heidegger calls "selfhood" the "trajectory and domain of owning-to [*Zu-eignung*] and of the origin of the 'to' [*zu*] and the 'self' [*sich*]" (C223; B317). This means that selfhood names an aspect of be-ing's occurrence as enowning, namely the "owning-to" through which humans find their "own," their "self." As the trajectory and domain of the "owning-to," selfhood is also "*the ground of belongingness to be-ing,*[10] which selfhood includes in itself the (inabiding) owning-over-to [*Über-eignung*]" (ibid.). Human's belongingness to be-ing originates in selfhood in that, in being owned-to

---

9. See the last chapter of this book titled "Be-ing."
10. Italics added.

their being, humans are owned-over-to the truth of be-ing. The terms "owning-to" and "owning-over-to" belong together and designate again the turning in enowning. In owning-to, being-t/here (*Da-sein*) is enowned by being owned-over-to the truth of be-ing as enowning. "Selfhood" is grounded in "own-hood" (*Eigen-tum*), i.e., the reigning of the owning (*Eignung*) in enowning (C224; B319f).

As a result, we find a double "foundation" for the human self: the human self is grounded in selfhood which originates in enownment. But this foundation does not mean that one occurrence is built over the other. Instead, one occurrence occurs *within* the other and neither of these occurrences can happen without the other. The coming to themselves of humans occurs within selfhood (owning-to and owning-over-to), and the reigning of selfhood occurs within enowning. At the same time, enowning occurs only through the coming to themselves of humans. By abiding in and thus remaining exposed to be-ing's withdrawal, into which they are set-out in the acknowledgment of the abandonment of being, humans let that withdrawal be, i.e., they provide a site for it, so that be-ing may occur as enowning. Being-t/here is owned-to (its occurring) through the inabiding of humans, an inabiding which, in turn, is owned-to humans in the grounding attunement of reservedness.

Abiding in the t/here, humans are grounded grounders of the openness of the abysmal truth of be-ing. They are grounders of this openness (being-t/here) by abiding in it; and they are grounded in that their abiding in being-t/here is owned to them out of be-ing's abysmal occurrence, to which they remain exposed.[11] In this exposure they find themselves and can truly be with themselves (*bei-sich*). Note, here, that Heidegger does not say that humans are themselves, but that they are *with* themselves. This expression "with themselves" has the sense both of nearness and distance which, as we will see, resonates also in the essential determinations that humans find when they are truly with themselves. Grounded historically in being-t/here, humans are called *"seekers," "preservers,"*

---

11. See also John Sallis, "Grounders of the Abyss," in *Companion to Heidegger's "Contributions to Philosophy,"* ed. Charles E. Scott, Susan M. Schoenbohm, Daniela Vallega-Neu, and Alejandro Vallega (Bloomington and Indianapolis: Indiana University Press, 2001), pp. 181–197.

and "*guardians* of the stillness of the passing of the last god." These determinations point to the ecstatic temporalities that constitute the care (be-
ing) of Dasein in *Being and Time* (C208; B294, section 171). But we
should be careful not to read them simply in relation to the future, past,
and present, and should keep in mind the circularity at play in ecstatic
temporality, where each ecstasy weaves into the other.

In section 38, Heidegger calls *seeking* an "already holding-oneself-in-
the-truth, in the open of self-concealment* and self-withdrawing," and
"the grounding relation to hesitating *refusal*" (C56; B80). As seekers,
humans remain exposed toward the self-concealment and self-refusal in
which be-ing sways. This seeking does not stand as a contrast to a finding but is in itself a finding, the finding of "what" conceals itself—of be-
ing. In seeking be-ing's self-concealment and in remaining attuned to
reservedness, humans keep this concealment exposed in *being-t/here*.

As seekers, humans are also *preservers* of the truth of being. The German word for "preserver," *Wahrer*, contains the root meaning *wahr*,
which means "true." Humans preserve the truth of being by holding it
open, by abiding in the t/here, which occurs, again, out of the grounding
attunement of reservedness. The preserving of the truth of be-ing in
which this truth is held in disclosure requires (as we will see in more detail
later) that it be sheltered in a being. This being the case, humans can be
preservers of the truth of being only by sheltering it in beings. The essential determination of humans as seekers points to the going ahead into be-
ing's self-withdrawal. Their determination as preservers points to their
holding open the clearing of be-ing's self-withdrawal. Without keeping
open this clearing, the withdrawal of be-ing would close itself within its
own self-secluding motion and disappear as such (which would be the ultimate end of the history of be-ing).

The third essential determination of humans as *guardians* gathers the
two previous determinations into the moment (*Augenblick*) of the passing
of the last god. This passing is discussed further in the last joining, "The
Last God." In the discussion of this last joining, we will see in more detail
how the passing of the last god marks the moment of the historical
grounding of the other beginning. The passing of the last god is a historical event that be-ing-historical thinking "only" attempts to prepare

through the grounding of the truth of be-ing in being-t/here. For Heidegger, the guarding of this moment also marks the highest destiny of human being.

To prepare the moment for the passing of the last god in grounding the truth of be-ing in being-t/here requires, for be-ing-historical think-ing, a mindfulness of this truth, a mindfulness which can only occur *as* thinking holds itself in this truth, attuned by reservedness.

c) The Truth of Be-ing: Abyss and Time-Space

The core section of the "Grounding" joining, in which Heidegger un-folds the swaying of truth, is certainly the rich and dense section 242 which will guide the following meditations. According to section 187, the primary sense of *ground* (in which ground as projecting-grounding is grounded) is the essential swaying of *truth*. In section 242, Heidegger says that the originary swaying of the ground—of truth—is the *abyss** (*Ab-grund*),[12] and he unfolds this abyss in thinking as time-space.

Reading this section we should keep in mind that what it says is thought and spoken in the transition from the first to the other beginning. Truth unfolds inceptively as abyss as thinking is set-out into the more originary domain of history in which the truth of be-ing occurs as refusal. Out of this refusal, be-ing-historical thinking finds itself enowned and be-longing to this abysmal occurrence of be-ing. This in-between of refusal and enowning, in which thinking finds itself as it thinks this occurrence, carries the intimation of an event that *is* not yet, an event in which, for a moment, be-ing would sway fully as enowning and would inaugurate an-other beginning of history.

In section 242, which unfolds the essential swaying of the truth of be-

---

12. I translate *"Abgrund"* as "abyss" and not as "ab-ground" as Emad and Maly do. It is true that—as they argue in the "Foreword" to *Contributions*—for Heidegger *"Ab-grund"* has a relation to *"Grund,"* i.e., to "ground." But, at the same time, the "bottomlessness" of the abyss remains an essential sense in the German *"Abgrund,"* which should resonate also in the English translation. The compelling distress that thinking experiences arises pre-cisely in the experience of the groundlessness of be-ing.

ing as enowning out of its inceptive occurrence as abyss, Heidegger writes, "The abyss* is the staying away of ground," while ground is "the self-concealing-receiving, because it is a sustaining—and this as a reaching-through* [*Durchragen*] of what is to be grounded. Ground: the self-conceal-ing* in the sustaining that reaches-through* [*im tragenden Durchragen*]" (C265; B379). Ground first opens in the transition from the first to the other beginning as a staying away of ground, as a lack of sustaining and reaching through as which ground sways. Instead of speaking of a "stay-ing away" of sustaining and reaching through, we could say "abandon-ment of being." What be-ing-historical thinking first experiences as it is set-out through startled dismay and awe into the originary occurrence of be-ing is that the truth of be-ing does not sway as ground, that it does not sustain and permeate beings, but that is has abandoned beings. But we should be aware that this ground that "stays away" has nothing to do with a metaphysically conceived ground or with a firm foundation since it al-ways essentially occurs as self-concealing. Ground is also in itself abys-mal when it sustains and permeates beings.

On the other hand, the refusal of ground as which truth as abyss first opens for being-historical thinking is not mere groundlessness, but re-mains related to ground. Heidegger is able to indicate this by italicizing the part of the German word for abyss which means "ground": "Ab-*grund*." Ground (-*grund*) is here understood as be-ing's self-concealing that sustains and reaches-through. Even the staying away of ground (be-ing's swaying as refusal) is related to ground by virtue of the open-ing which occurs in it. "Not granting [*Versagung*] is not nothing but rather an outstanding originary manner of letting *be* unfulfilled, of let-ting *be* empty—thus an outstanding manner of opening* [*Eröffnung*]" (C265; B379). This means that the letting be unfulfilled is a manner of disclosure. This disclosure, says Heidegger, is not simple indefinite emptiness but is "definite" (*bestimmt*). It is pertinent that *Stimmung*, "attunement," resonates in the German word for "definite," *bestimmt*. The determination of the openness released in the refusal of ground arises in an attunement that characterizes the openness. Since in the abyss ground still sways, even though it does not properly (*eigentlich*) ground (in which case be-ing would sway fully as enowning and beings would no longer be abandoned by be-ing), this ground dwells in a *hesitation* (*Zögerung*). In be-ing-historical thinking in the transition from the first to the other beginning, ground (i.e., the truth of be-ing) is experienced and thought as *"hesitating self-refusal"* (*zögerndes Sichversagen*). The hesitation marks the "still" (of the first beginning) and "not yet" (of the other beginning), the temporalizing in-between of the first and the other beginning in which the truth of be-ing unfolds in thinking. We encountered the hesitating self-refusal previously in the discussion of the cleft in which the truth of be-ing first opens up in the leap. One moment of the cleft of be-ing is its remaining in itself, which is the self-refusal as which be-ing sways. But we have seen also that this remaining in itself, this bending back into nothingness, is understood as ripeness, as the not yet of gift and dissemination (*Verschenkung*). This moment of not yet resonates in the hesitation of be-ing's refusal through which the abyss remains related to the swaying of truth as enowning ground.

The experience of the truth of be-ing as hesitating self-refusal discloses the swaying of be-ing as enowning, which Heidegger calls *primordial ground* (*Ur-grund*). "For hesitating refusal is the hint by which *being-t/here* [. . .] is beckoned; and that is the resonance of the turning between 'the call' and belongingness, en-*ownment*, be-ing itself" (C265; B380). The word *"hint"* gathers the twofold temporality of the "still" and "not yet" that marks the abysmal truth as hesitating self-refusal. Its beckoning is the enowning call (the compelling distress) which lets humans belong to this truth by *being* the t/here, by abiding in the truth that opens out of the refusal of ground in the abyss. Be-ing as enowning sways out of the opening which is cleared in the hesitating self-refusal of be-ing. The primordial ground (enowning) arises out of the abyss (be-ing's self-refusal).

The primordial ground, i.e., enowning that arises in the abyss, determines and attunes (*bestimmt*) the "emptiness" that is cleared in the abyss.

> Enowning attunes—through and through—the essential swaying of truth. The openness of clearing of concealing* is thus originarily not a mere emptiness of not-being-occupied, but rather the attuned and attuning emptiness of the abyss*, which in accordance with the attuning hint of enowning is an attuned—and that means here an enjoined [*gefügter*]—abyss*. (C266; B381)

In the enowning that occurs out of the attuned-attuning abyss, being-t/here, humans, and gods are enowned. The t/here is the opening cleared in the abyss; humans are enowned in reservedness to be in this opening and the gods are enowned out of the abyss in the undecidability of their coming or leaving.[13] Heidegger unfolds the mutual penetration of ground as abyss and of ground as enowning in thinking the "emptiness" that is cleared in the abyss and out of which humans and gods are enowned as *time-space*. The emptiness cleared in the abyss is, as we have seen, the t/here of being-t/here. Thus, time-space is a determination of the t/here *(Da)* of being-t/here in which the truth of be-ing (ground) is cleared as abyss.

> Self-refusal creates not only the *emptiness* of deprivation and awaiting but also, along with these, the emptiness that as an emptiness is in itself re-moving [*entrückend*], removing into coming to be* [*Künftigkeit*] and thus at the same time breaking open what has been [*Gewesendes*], which, as it meets what is coming to be makes up the present as moving into aban-donment, but as remembering-awaiting [abandonment].* (C268; B383)

The temporalization *(Zeitigung)* of the time-space gathers three re-movals* *(Entrückungen)*, the removal into coming to be, the removal into having been, and the removal into the present abandonment of be-ing. They are gathered in the moment *(Augenblick)* of the decision of be-ing, of be-ing's swaying as enowning or/and as refusal. The moment is in itself the domain of decision; as "remembering-awaiting," the mo-ment gathers the in-between of the first and the other beginning in which the being-historical thinking of *Contributions* moves.

The temporalizing (the "time-") of the time-space occurs as a removal into be-ing's self-refusal. But, at the same time, this refusal is held in a hesi-tation; only in this hesitation is an opening (the t/here) cleared. This hesi-tation is where *spatializing (Räumung)* comes into play. In hesitation, the removal into self-refusal occurs as an *enrapturing* *(Berückung)* that

13. "What opens itself for concealment* *(Verbergung)* is originarily the remoteness of undecidabilty whether the* god moves away from or toward us. That is to say: In this remoteness and its undecidability is manifest the concealment* of that which we, follow-ing this opening,* call god" (C267; B382). The undecidability of the coming or leaving of the gods is gathered in the hint through which, in hesitating withdrawal, the enowning attunes and determines the opening of the abyss.

Heidegger calls "encircling hold" (*Umhalt*). The German word "*Berück-ung*" denotes ec-stasis, being set-out of everydayness, as well as being held in a magical circle, as when one is enchanted. Both an opening and a delimitation occur which have no familiar ground. Where the temporalizing tends into self-refusal, spatializing offers the possibility of gifting [*Schenk-ung*]. "Enrapturing* is the spatializing of enowning" (C268; B384).

The gathering of the removing into abandonment (temporalizing) is a counter-movement to the enrapturing as encircling hold (spatializing). And yet temporalizing occurs only in spatializing and vice versa. Withdrawal occurs and is only in hesitation. Hesitation occurs only in the tension to the withdrawal. "As the onefold of originary temporalizing and spatializing, time-space is itself originarily the site of[14] the moment* [*Augenblicksstätte*]" (ibid.). The site of the moment is the site of the moment of decision of the first and the other beginning. This site of the moment of decision (the t/here of the truth of be-ing) is what the be-ing-historical thinking of *Contributions* attempts to ground. But this is possible only through the sheltering of the t/here in beings.

d) Sheltering the Truth of Be-ing in Beings

In metaphysics, the truth of being is concealed "behind" the appearance of beings. Being withdraws as it brings beings to presence. It withdraws most decisively at the end of metaphysics in the domination of machination and lived experience when beings are abandoned by being and being remains forgotten. In the other beginning—if it occurs—beings *shelter* the truth of being. In German, "sheltering," *Bergung*, has the sense of "rescuing" and "bringing something to safety" into a secure and possibly also concealed place. Thus, beings are thought to provide a sheltered "place" for the truth of be-ing, i.e., for be-ing's occurrence as unconcealing-concealing, so that be-ing may occur in and through these sheltering beings. These beings shelter not only the presencing (*Anwesen*) in which they come to appearance, but, above all, the concealment that

14. "Of" again used as "double genitive."

belongs to the truth of be-ing. "Sheltering also definitely moves* the self-concealment* [*Sichverbergen*] into the opening*, in the same way in which it is itself permeated by the *clearing* of self-concealment" (C272; B390). In the sheltering of the truth of be-ing in beings, the occurrence of truth as unconcealing-concealing permeates these beings, echoes in their being. At the same time, this sheltering is not something which comes after truth is disclosed. Truth can disclose itself in being-t/here only if it (truth) is sheltered in a being. In this sheltering, truth finds a concrete historical site. Throughout *Contributions*, Heidegger names several beings that may shelter the truth of be-ing: thing, tool, work, deed, word, sacrifice, gaze, and even machination[15] (C48; B70. C290; B413). In being-historical thinking, the beings that shelter truth (the truth which emerges in thinking) are words. If *Contributions* is able to say the truth of be-ing, i.e., to disclose it to the reader, this entails that this truth is sheltered in the words in which it is written.

Contributions dedicates only a few pages to the question of sheltering. But in these pages we find several references to Heidegger's essay "The Origin of the Work of Art." As Heidegger indicates in section 247, the question of "The Origin of the Work of Art" belongs in the domain of the grounding of being-t/here and the trajectories of sheltering truth (C274; B392). It develops in more detail the question of sheltering with reference to special modes of sheltering that initiate another beginning of history. Heidegger attributes this possibility especially to art. He considers how a work of art (a painting, a temple, the word of the poet) shelters the truth of be-ing insofar as it discloses and preserves the occurrence of truth. At the same time, Heidegger's essay is itself an attempt at a sheltering by thinking and by saying an originary, inceptive sheltering. Therefore, we may distinguish two different shelterings at work in Heidegger's thinking and saying: one mode is the transitory (*übergänglich*) sheltering which occurs in Heidegger's writing, while the other mode is the inceptive sheltering of the other beginning of history which

---

15. The fact that Heidegger thinks of utensils and machination as modes of sheltering points to the possibility of thinking something like a transformed everydayness in the other beginning, as well as a transformed relation between be-ing and technology.

the be-ing-historical thinking of *Contributions* attempts to prepare by projecting open and, thus, grounding in thinking being-t/here, the clearing of the truth of be-ing. The transitory sheltering of *Contributions* is inceptive, too, but it also stands in the shadow of the first beginning. The struggle which Heidegger has in attempting to write from enowning becomes manifest, for instance, in section 41 where he writes:

> Every saying of be-ing is kept in words and namings which, if* they are understood* in the direction of everyday references to beings and are thought exclusively in this direction, are misconstruable as the utterance of being.* Therefore it is not as if what is needed first is the failure of the question (within the domain of thinking-interpretation of be-ing), but the word itself already discloses something (familiar) and thus hides that which has to be brought into the open through thinking-saying. (C58; B83)

This indicates how the question of sheltering the truth of be-ing in a word does not depend simply on someone finding the right word. Every word discloses something familiar and consequently may be understood only according to these familiar ways. This means, in our case, that every word may be understood in metaphysical ways which give priority to the representation of entities. This suggests that no saying can escape the possibility of being misunderstood, i.e., of concealing truth instead of sheltering it. For thinking to be able to say be-ing in a way which shelters truth, it needs an appropriate listening, i.e., a listening which remains attuned to the occurrence of truth which the words disclose. The words, on the other hand, can bring the occurrence of truth to the open only in a thinking-saying which is enowned by the truth of be-ing itself. This is indicated by the expression used in "The Origin of the Work of Art": "truth's setting-itself-into-work" (*das Sich-ins-Werk-setzen der Wahrheit*). Truth sets itself into work by enowning being-t/here and compelling humans to be the t/here by sheltering the t/here in a work.

Truth cannot occur without being grounded in being-t/here by being sheltered in a being. But, despite Heidegger's understanding of the "simultaneity" of be-ing and beings, there remains a *difference between the truth of be-ing and beings*.[16] In bending back into itself (in its clefting),

---

16. See section 268 of *Contributions*.

the truth of being keeps itself in an excessive reserve with respect to beings that shelter truth, even if they are not secondary to its occurrence
but are part of it, occur *in* it. The difference between the truth of be-ing
and beings is further accentuated, in *Contributions*, when Heidegger as-
serts that truth cannot put itself directly into a being but first must be
transformed into the *strife of world and earth*.

> The occurrence [*self-concealing*] is transformed and preserved (why) in
> the strife of *earth and world*. The strifing of the strife puts truth into
> work—into tool—experiences truth as thing, accomplishes truth in
> deed and sacrifice.* (C273; B391)

"The Origin of the Work of Art" elaborates in more detail the relation
between truth, the strife of the world and earth, and beings (works of
art), something which cannot be done in this short introduction. In this
essay, Heidegger calls the world "the self-opening *openness* of the broad
paths of the simple and essential decisions in the destiny of a historical
people," and the earth "the spontaneous forthcoming of that which is
continually self-secluding and to that extent sheltering and concealing"
(GA 5, p. 35). The world opens historical paths while the earth secludes
itself and thus shelters. They occur against each other and yet only
through each other: Earth can only emerge as self-secluding in a world,
while the world needs earth as that on which it can ground its historical
paths. This strife of world and earth is grounded in what Heidegger
calls *"primordial strife"* (*Urstreit*), which is the occurrence of truth as
unconcealing-concealing. The primordial strife as which truth occurs
is, in a sense, more originary than the strife of world and earth, even if
there is no truth without the strife of world and earth through which
truth is sheltered in beings. In its self-concealment (self-refusal), truth
bears possibility in the sense of capacity (*Vermögen*) which exceeds the
specific historical disclosure and concealment in the strife of earth and
world. This is why there are many possibilities in which the truth of be-
ing unfolds historically. Some are known to us through Heidegger's
reading of the history of Western philosophy: the truth of be-ing discloses and conceals itself first in *phusis*, in *ousia*, in the medieval *substan-*

tia creata, in presentedness (*Vorgestelltheit*) of subjectivity, and finally in machination (in a narrow sense).[17]

Truth is sheltered in beings through the strife of world and earth. At the same time, the strife of world and earth needs beings in order to occur; it needs a particular sheltering if it is to occur as such. The hint for this sheltering arises out of the primordial strife, out of the concealment which, in the end of metaphysics, occurs as refusal of its essential swaying and compels being-t/here in order to occur as such. The t/here of the truth of being needs humans to abide in it, to be the opening by way of its sheltering in beings. Human being has a particular role in the sheltering of truth; it finds its essence precisely in this sheltering which occurs in two fundamental modes which in "The Origin of the Work of Art" Heidegger calls "creating" (*Schaffen*) and "preserving" (*Bewahren*).

The sheltering of the truth of be-ing does *not* occur *either* in creating *or* in preserving but in both modes. Inceptively, creating and preserving are not something human subjects do. They occur in the turning of enowning through a fundamental attunement in which humans respond to the call arising in the truth of being, a call which is heard *as* creating or preserving occur. In creating, truth is brought into a being as it occurs, for instance, in painting, sculpting, or poetizing. But preserving is just as essential. It occurs when somebody is unsettled by a work of art or by words and experiences, in this unsettling, be-ing as such.

Accordingly, the importance of art and poetry for Heidegger is manifest. In the preparation of the other beginning, the other beginning in which the truth of be-ing as enowning would inaugurate another historical epoch, art and poetry—and also, of course, thinking—have an essential role in their capacity to move humans in an essential way. No doubt Heidegger found himself moved in such a way by Hölderlin's poetry. But more humans need to be unsettled into the abysmal truth of be-ing in order for the other beginning to arise epochally; the truth of be-ing needs the ones to come.

---

17. One could examine how the truth of be-ing also unfolds in the strife of world and earth in non-Western history in Asian, African, or native American Indian thought.

7. THE ONES TO COME

The ones to come are those humans who, attuned by reservedness, respond to the distress of be-ing and thereby become grounders of the essential occurrence of truth. The role that humans play in the grounding of truth in being-t/here has to some extent already been discussed, especially in the "Grounding" joining.[1] We have seen how, through abiding in the t/here, humans become seekers, preservers, and guardians of the truth of be-ing. The issue now is to understand the designation of humans who ground the truth of be-ing by sheltering it in beings as *the ones to come*. As we will see, they acquire this designation in relation to the "last god."

The ones to come are not so called because they might come in a possible future. Even if Heidegger says that the ones to come, the grounders of the other beginning, first "need to be prepared" (C277; B395), he also says that "today there are already a few of those who are to come" (C280; B400). The futurity which resonates in their name echoes the original temporality which Heidegger elaborates in *Being and Time* as the way the being of Dasein occurs. It names a coming toward which occurs together with having been and presencing. Now, however, the horizon out of which this temporalizing occurs is conceived in relation to the distancing and nearing of the gods. So it is that Heidegger calls the grounders of the other beginning the ones *to come (Zu-künftige)* because they are those *toward whom comes (zu-kommt)* "the hint and onset of distancing and nearing of the last god" (C277; B395).

The "hint of the distancing *and* nearing of the last god" designates the moment of decision over the other beginning of history. The hint gathers temporality in that it occurs both as one arrives and as one departs. It gathers arising and departing, nearing and distancing in their decision. At the same time, the hint of the nearing and distancing of the last god arises

1. b) "Being-T/here—Selfhood—Humans."

in being-t/here, i.e., out of the disclosed occurrence of the truth of be-ing. The occurrence of the distancing *and* nearing of the last god is intimately connected with the unfolding of truth as time-space; they echo both the original spatializing (nearing) and the original temporalizing (distancing), which are gathered in their unity in the moment (*Augenblick*) that marks the decision of the other beginning of the history of be-ing.

As those to whom the hint of the last god comes, the ones to come closely attend to the distancing and nearing, and, so, become "the stillest witness to the stillest stillness, in which an imperceptible tug turns the truth back, out of the confusion of all calculated correctness into its essential sway* [*in ihr Wesen*]: keeping sheltered and concealed* [*verborgen*] what is most concealed* [*das Verborgenste*], the trembling* [*Erzitterung*] in the passing of the decision of gods, the essential swaying of be-ing" (C277; B395). The ones to come become grounders of the truth of be-ing, not by some action they perform as subjects, but by witnessing in stillness the passing of the decision of the gods. Nonetheless, this witnessing is not mere passivity; the German word for "witness" is "*Zeuge*," derived from "*zeugen*," which means not only "to witness," "to bear testimony," but also "to procreate." The witnessing of the stillness in which the passage of the gods is decided allows this passage to occur. In this context, stillness does not mean motionlessness but its opposite, a most intense motion[2] which culminates in an intense vibration, in a trembling (*Erzitterung*) which marks the moment of the decision of the gods and the inceptive swaying of be-ing. This also means that the decision that marks the grounding of the other beginning does not have the character of a grandiose or glamorous event. It occurs, imperceptible to a detached observer, in the stillest stillness.

The ones to come are thought in relation to the decision of the other beginning of Western history, which occurs in the passing of the last god. If, on the one hand, this decision first needs to be prepared, on the other

---

2. The reader may compare this "stillness" to the passage in "The Origin of the Work of Art" where Heidegger writes, "Where rest [*Ruhe*] includes motion, there can exist a repose which is an inner concentration of motion, hence supreme agitation, assuming that the mode of motion requires such a rest" (*Basic Writings*, trans. David Farrell Krell [San Francisco: Harper San Francisco, 1992], p. 173.).

hand, this preparation already partakes in that decision in that it opens its possibility. This points to the double sense of "inceptive" or "inceptuality" (*Anfänglichkeit*) at play in *Contributions:* While the other beginning first needs to be prepared through the projecting-grounding of being-t/here, this projecting-grounding is attuned by what is to be prepared and thereby begins the other beginning. Correspondingly, the ones to come are both those who first prepare the time-space for the decision over the other beginning of history in the passing of the last god *and* those who witness this passing (who first need to be prepared). Heidegger also characterizes the ones to come who first open and prepare the time-space for the decision of be-ing as *those who go under* (*die Untergehenden*). Those who go under take the first inceptive leap into the other beginning in the transition from the first to the other beginning.

> *Our hour is the epoch of going-under.*
> Taken in its essential sense, going-under means going along the path of the reticent preparing for those who are to come, for the moment, and for the site, in all of which the decision of the arrival and staying-away of gods falls. This going-under is the very first of the first beginning.
> [...]
> Those who *are going-under* in the essential sense are those who undergo* [*unter-laufen*] what is coming (what is futural) and sacrifice themselves to it as its future invisible ground.[3] (C278; B397)

Heidegger not only differentiates the ones to come who go under from the ones to come who witness the passing of the last god. For Heidegger, the decision of the other beginning also entails different stages from the going-under of a few who first open the time-space, and thereby the possibility (*Vermögen*) of the decision of the other beginning of the history of be-ing, to the moment when an entire people are grounded in this other beginning. This is what section 45 from the "Preview" of *Contributions* suggests. The title of this section is "The 'Decision.'" The decision at stake here is the main decision that motivates and frames *Contributions*,

3. In the last joining, "The Ones To Come," Heidegger names those who prepare the ones to come "those who are on the way back [*die Rückwegigen*]"; they are "those who find, traverse, and build the way back from the experienced abandonment of being" (C289; B410f).

the decision between history and the loss of history, i.e., between an ultimate concealment of be-ing's historicality (*Geschichtlichkeit*) at the end of
the first beginning and the opening of the other beginning of Western history. This decision, says Heidegger here, is made by "the *granting* or *staying away* of those outstanding marked ones* [*ausgezeichnete Gezeichnete*]
that we call 'the ones to come' " (C66; B96). These "ones to come" emerge
in three steps which do not arrive in a regular linear sequence (although
some linearity is suggested by the way Heidegger enumerates them), but
overlap and intertwine. They lead both to a greater number of "ones to
come" and to a greater achievement in the grounding of the other beginning of history.

First come "*those few individuals*" who ground in advance in poetry,
thinking, action, and who sacrifice the sites which open the possibility for
sheltering truth, a sheltering in which being-t/here becomes historical.
These are the ones who go under. We can safely assume that Heidegger
would count among these few individuals at least himself and Hölderlin.[4]
Next come "*those many allied ones*" who grasp the will and grounding of
the few individuals (i.e., they are allied with those few individuals) and
make it visible in their deeds (presumably in thinking, poetizing, art, gestures, etc.). What marks the next group of "ones to come" is that for them
the grounding of the truth of enowning achieves durability or steadfastness. Heidegger calls them "*those many who are interrelated* by their common historical (earth- and world-bound) origins" (C67; B96). However,
they do not yet mark the completed beginning of the other beginning.
They, too, like the few individuals who first open the time-space of decision and the allied ones who sustain this inceptive opening, "still stand
partly in the old and current and planned orders*" (C67; B97). The "futurity" of the ones to come implies that they stand "ahead," or are attuned
and determined by what is not yet.

Contingent upon the preparation provided by the few individuals,
the many allied, and the many interrelated ones to come, Heidegger en-

---

4. The designation, "those who go under," recalls, of course, Nietzsche's *Thus Spoke Zar-
athustra;* while section 105 of *Contributions* suggests that Kierkegaard, too, reaches inceptively into the decision over be-ing's historicality.

visions the possibility of the historical grounding of a people (*Volk*). This would be the moment when the other beginning would actually be the beginning of a new epoch of Western history. Heidegger is never more explicit or concrete about how this other beginning of the history of a people develops. It certainly cannot be imagined but only intimated in its possibility by those who find themselves already enowned and who abide in being-t/here, i.e. by the ones to come.

For Heidegger, the ones to come relate essentially to the passing of the last god to which is dedicated the last joining of *Contributions,* and which, together with the other five joinings, marks the realm in which being-historical thinking moves in transition from the first to the other beginning of the history of be-ing.

8. THE LAST GOD

Dann feiern das Brautfest Menschen und Götter
Es feiern die Lebenden all,
Und ausgeglichen
Ist eine Weile das Schicksal[1]

We have already looked at some preliminary determinations of the last god. It, the last god, is thought, in *Contributions*, as a temporal occurrence which occurs as a decision. Its decisive occurrence announces itself in a hint (a hinting) out of the withdrawal of be-ing, a withdrawal which thinking, attuned by startled dismay and awe, experiences in the acknowledgment of the abandonment of being and to which it remains exposed in the grounding leap into the abysmal disclosure of be-ing.

In section 256 Heidegger writes:

> The last god has its *essential swaying* within the hint, the onset and staying-away of the arrival as well as the flight of the gods who have been, and within their hidden* [*verborgenen*] transformation. The last god is not enowning itself; rather, it needs enowning as that to which the founder of the t/here [*Dagründer*] belongs. (C288; B409)

We begin by considering what the last god is not. It is not a higher being, not a "person" in any sense. It is not the creator of being, nor the "enowner" of be-ing, nor does it stand in any other way higher than being. In fact, the last god is regarded as needing enowning, i.e., as needing being. Of course this expression, "the last god needs being," does not mean that there is an entity (god) that needs enowning. The needing of the last god is not separate from or an attribute of its swaying. The god sways in a hinting, and this hinting occurs out of a need in which the god first becomes manifest for thinking. This means that there is not a god that hints but that the god/s become/s manifest *in* the hinting.

1. Friedrich Hölderlin, "Der Rhein."

We have explored briefly in the previous joining, "The Ones to Come," how the hint gathers nearing and distancing of the gods, which relates to the unfolding of the time-space of the truth of be-ing. In fact, in section 255 Heidegger says:

> In the sway of hinting lies the mystery of the unity* [Einheit] of the inner-most nearing in the utmost distancing, the* traversing of the widest free play of the time-space of be-ing. This utmost essential swaying of be-ing requires the innermost distress of abandonment by being. (C287; B408)

In the hint lies the traversing (*Ausmessung*), and this means a measuring through, an opening in its extremities of the moment and site (the t/here) of the truth of be-ing. For thinking, this opening occurs inceptively in the experience of the distress of the abandonment by being of machination-ally disclosed beings. The relation between the experience of the distress of the abandonment of being and the traversing of the time-space of the truth of be-ing is not simply one of a sequence in a linear time. Rather, the hint, in its traversing quality, is sheltered in the distress.

We encountered this relation between the experience of the distress of the abandonment of being and the traversing of the time-space of the truth of be-ing before, in the "Leap" joining, in the discussion of the cleft. The "cleft" names the truth of be-ing in its most inceptive swaying as re-fusal, and, at the same time, bears within it the widest traversing of truth in the direction of the gods on the one side and humans on the other. The hinting of the last god befalls humans only if they experience the utmost distress out of be ing's utmost self refusal. Bearing this distress by abid-ing in the clearing of be-ing's self-refusal, humans find themselves an-swering a call through which the hinting of the last god occurs. Enowning enowns humans *through* this call (*Zuruf*) that *is,* says Heidegger, "befall-ing *and* staying away" (ibid.). It is simultaneously both since it carries in it be-ing's essential swaying both as refusal *and* as compelling enowning[2] in the decision over "arrival or flight of gods and their places of mastery" (C287; B408). To summarize how the notions "enowning," "call," "hint," and "god/s" relate: enowning occurs as the enownment of being-

2. "Hint is hesitating self-refusal" (Section 242, C268; B383).

t/here in the turning in-between, between enowning call and enowned response (through humans' abiding in the t/here). In the enowning call occurs the hint of the last god which gathers both arrival and flight of the gods. The hinting is not yet the passing of the last god, which would mark the decision over be-ing's historical occurring, but opens in the cleft of be-ing the capacity (*Vermögen*) of that decision.

The hint as which the last god sways gathers a "plurality" of gods in the undecidedness—which does not mean decisionlessness—of their arrival or flight. Here the question arises: How does the singularity of the last god relate to the plurality of the gods? The plurality of the gods, says Heidegger, marks "the inner richness of the grounds and abysses in the site of* the moment [*Augenblicksstätte*] of the shining and concealing* of the hint of the last god" (C289; B411). In order to understand what this means, we should reconsider what grounding implies, namely, the occurring of the abysmal truth of be-ing through its sheltering in a being, a sheltering that provides a site for a particular historical opening (t/here) in which a world and an earth disclose. The grounding of be-ing—and this means be-ing itself—needs sheltering, and the god who needs be-ing needs this grounding. Only through a sheltering-grounding can the hint of the last god occur both transitionally as decision that is initiated but still undecided and with respect to the grounding that would mark the historical other beginning for a people. In other words, the hint of the last god is *not* a *transcendent* occurrence beyond beings but occurs only through beings. Since the modes of sheltering truth are manifold and they occur as a sheltering of unconcealment *and* concealment of be-ing, the hint of the god accordingly occurs in this manifoldness of modes of sheltering which preserve also the concealment that belongs to the occurrence of be-ing.

The plurality of the gods in their arrival and/or flight points to this manifoldness of modes of sheltering. At the same time, Heidegger conceives the plurality of gods, which occurs through manifold ways of sheltering the truth of be-ing, as ways in which the "one" last god sways, the passing of which initiates the other beginning of Western history. This "oneness" of the last god does not mean the oneness of an entity. The fact that the last god sways in flight and the arrival of a plurality of gods indicates that its singularity is not like the singularity of an entity, but instead marks the singularity of an event that cannot be understood as a kind of entity. The singular event in question is, of course, the decision of the other beginning of history. And, as we have seen in the joining "The Ones to Come," according to Heidegger, this beginning occurs in a process which remains mostly hidden and probably spans centuries; and it is not clear at all whether this other beginning will ever gain the consistency which will definitely put the first beginning behind itself. In other words, it is not clear whether the passing of the last god will ever occur. It remains in decision in the inceptive and transitional thought of *Contributions*, and it is from this decision-character that it gets its designation as being the *last* (*letzter*).

The last, says Heidegger in section 253, "is that which not only needs but which *is* itself the longest going-ahead* [*Vorläuferschaft*, 'fore-runnership']: not the ceasing, but the deepest beginning, which reaches out the furthest and catches up with itself with the greatest of difficulty"* (C285; B405). "Last," then, does not mean last in a chain of events and therefore "end." Rather, Heidegger thinks "last" with respect to the inceptive character of the swaying of gods. It gathers the same double temporality as the word "beginning" in the "other beginning." "Beginning" means both the one beginning (i.e., the originary inceptive occurrence of be-ing in its truth, which occurs also in the first beginning) and the beginning again (in an *other* way) in a more futural sense, but of a "future," a coming to be, that is already t/here, that *is* in being not yet. The word "last" also refers to the utmost refusal, i.e., the most originary "not" of be-ing out of which alone the hint of the last god can become manifest. "The *last* god is not an end but rather the beginning as it sways into itself* [*Insicheinschwingen*] and thus the highest shape of not-granting" (C293; B416). The last god sways in the not-granting, i.e., in the utmost refusal and at the same time in the farthest going ahead.

The originary temporality (a coming to be which occurs in having been) that marks the word "last" is also at play in the word "passing" (*Vorbeigang*). Heidegger conceives of the other beginning of Western history as the occurrence of the passing of the last god, and not simply of its presencing or appearing. This passing occurs in stillness. We have seen in the joining "The Ones To Come" how this stillness occurs as a most intense motion, a trembling (*Erzitterung*) that gathers coming to be and passing away in the decision of a moment (*Augenblick*).

Stillness, for Heidegger, also indicates the origin of language, in the wider sense in which he exposes language in "The Origin of the Work of Art," i.e., not only as spoken or written language, but as an opening articulation of be-ing which occurs in any originary mode of sheltering.[3] This sheltering occurs through the ones to come who stay attuned especially to the withdrawal of be-ing and who respond to the need of the gods which resounds out of this withdrawal, i.e., in the echo of be-ing. In "The Origin of the Work of Art," Heidegger also notes that even though all sheltering of truth in creating and preserving occurs through language (he calls all sheltering "poetry" (*Dichtung*) in a larger sense), poetry, in a narrow sense, maintains a priority over the other modes of sheltering. As mentioned earlier, for Heidegger, the poet is the one on whom the hint of the gods befalls first and who passes on the hinting of the gods in his poetry (GA 39, p. 32). The poet veils (*"hüllt,"* which has the sense of sheltering and of concealing) the hinting of the gods in words, and thinking puts what the words of the poet shelter into the light of concepts (GA 39, p. 286). For Heidegger, the one poet who reaches furthest in the saying of the gods is Hölderlin; consequently, we are called to understand Heidegger's thinking-saying of the gods in relation to his dialogue with Hölderlin.[4]

"The Last God" is the last joining of *Contributions,* a joining that comes last in the sense we have explicated, namely, that it reaches furthest into the beginning. The hint of the last god emerges out of the echo of be-ing in the distress of being's utmost abandonment. Thus, with the last joining we turn "back" to the first joining, which is not merely the first step in a sequence of events that thinking traverses, but which already opens the whole domain of the truth of be-ing as enowning which each joining unfolds anew from a different angle. Within *Contributions,* we find many passages where Heidegger attempts to present the joinings together, and this means the "whole" occurrence of enowning as it comes to thinking and is articulated in the transitory but also inceptive thinking of *Contributions.* We will consider one of these attempts in the following.

---

3. Heidegger, *Basic Writings,* trans. David Farrell Krell (San Francisco: Harper San Francisco, 1992), p. 198.
4. This means that a thorough interpretation of the gods in Heidegger's *Contributions* needs to take into consideration Heidegger's Hölderlin lecture courses.

9. BE-ING

The last part of *Contributions*, entitled "Be-ing," was written after the other parts of the book, in an attempt to rethink the entire jointure of the truth of be-ing. In that same attempt, we will look more closely at section 267, where Heidegger unfolds enowning in the manifoldness of the events it carries within it. These events include the enownment of being-t/here, the enownment of gods and humans in their encounter, enowning with respect to the difference between be-ing and beings, and the occurring of these enownments in "simpleness," "uniqueness," and "aloneness." While the six joinings that structure *Contributions* unfold enowning primarily in the transition from metaphysics to being-historical thinking by emphasizing the transformation which human being and thinking undergo, in section 267 Heidegger unfolds enowning out of the distress of the gods. This does not mean that in the end Heidegger gives priority to the gods over being and humans. As he says in section 259 (also from the last part of *Contributions*), "understanding be-ing-historical thinking from within the perspective of gods is 'the same' as attempting to indicate what is ownmost to this thinking from within the perspective of humans*" (C309; B439).

The way Heidegger opens section 267 indicates that he considers this section (perhaps more than most) to be a thinking-saying from enowning: "Be-ing is *en-owning*. This word names be-ing in thinking and grounds be-ing's essential swaying in its own jointure, which lets itself be indicated in the manifoldness of enownings" (C330f; B470). These enownings are not separate occurrences so much as they are different aspects of one occurrence, the essential swaying of the truth of be-ing as enowning. Heidegger develops eight aspects of enowning, each of which, he says, thinks the occurrence of be-ing "entirely" (*ganz*), i.e., they do not develop parts of be-ing as enowning (as if one could divide this occurrence into separate parts), nor are the enownings able to say be-ing fully (*voll*), since the full saying of enowning would require that we are able to think all its aspects at once, which is impossible—at least for the transitory thinking of *Contributions* (C332; B471).

As we follow Heidegger through the eight enownings, we should keep in mind, again, that they do not mark a sequence in a linear time and that, even though enowning is unfolded out of the need of the gods, the articulation of enowning in this section occurs as it is thought in the attunement of reservedness; it occurs out of *being-t/here* in that abysmal opening of be-ing into which thinking finds itself unsettled in the acknowledgment of the abandonment of being. The first enowning says:

> 1. *en-ownment,* namely that, in the needfulness out of which gods need be-ing, this be-ing necessitates being-t/here* for* [*zur*]¹ the grounding of be-ing's own truth and thus lets the 'between' [*Zwischen*], the enownment of being-t/here* through [*durch*]² gods and owning of gods to themselves, hold sway as en-owning. (C331; B470)

As in "Echo," the jointure of en-owning arises in a needfulness. But whereas in the "Echo" joining this needfulness is unfolded in the direction of the abandonment and forgetfulness of being, here it is articulated, prior to the articulation of beings and humans, as the needfulness "out of which" gods need be-ing. Gods are not revealed to inceptual thinking prior to their need of be-ing but announce themselves for the be-ing-historical thinking of *Contributions* in the need. Thinking experiences this need of the gods to necessitate being-t/here, i.e., the inceptual opening of the truth of be-ing as withdrawal. In turn, through this opening—as it discloses inceptively—gods in their need first find a site of be-ing and, therefore, are owned to themselves (*zu ihnen selbst zugeeingnet*).

This first moment of the disclosure of the truth of be-ing in the enownment of the in-between, i.e., of being-t/here, implies the second aspect of enowning, the decision of gods and humans:

---

1. "*Zur* Gründung" means that being-t/here is enowned *in order* for the truth of be-ing to sway as ground.
2. By translating "*durch*" as "by," as Emad and Maly do, the reader may be misled into thinking that the gods are the ones who enown being-t/here. But, as explained in the previous chapter, "The Last God," gods are not the "enowners" of being-t/here; instead, through their call, being-t/here is enowned if humans respond to the call by abiding in the t/here.

2. The enowning of en-ownment gathers within itself the *de-cision* [*Ent-scheidung*]: that freedom, as the abysmal ground*, lets a distress emerge from out of which, as from out of the overflow of the ground, gods and man come forth into partedness. (Ibid.)

Gods and humans are *de-cided*, i.e., they are parted as they come forth in being-t/here out of a distress. This distress dwells in the needfulness of the gods which necessitates being-t/here (first aspect of enowning) and is now further articulated as originating in freedom—the abysmal ground—and as being the "overflow" of this ground. Freedom names the swaying of truth itself[3] which opens as the abyss out of which enowning occurs, i.e., the overflow of the ground, which lets gods and humans come forth (enowns) in their partedness.

Where gods announce themselves in the necessitating of being-t/here, humans emerge as those who, attuned by the abysmal event of the truth of be-ing, need to *be* the t/here, to hold open the opening of the abysmal truth of be-ing. Humans emerge—in partedness from the gods—as those who respond to the need that originates in the abysmal truth of be-ing. But why do they come forth in their partedness?

Gods dwell in their absence, in their needfulness of be-ing. Being-t/here does not result in the presencing of the gods but rather opens a time-space in which their flight and arrival becomes manifest. In being the t/here, humans come to be who they are in "resisting" the withdrawal of this opening of truth as they abide in it. They become grounders of a time-space for the manifestation of the gods in the gods' "not yet" and "not any more" precisely by resisting the withdrawal in which they (the gods) dwell and, therefore, by parting from them. This entails that gods and humans in their partedness (which remains a part*ing*) stay essentially related, and this is what the third aspect of enowning addresses:

3. En-ownment as de-cision brings to the parted ones *countering*, namely that this "toward-each-other" of the broadest needful de-cision must stand in the utmost "counter," because it bridges over the abyss of the needed be-ing. (Ibid.)

---

3. Compare Heidegger's essay "On the Essence of Ground," in *Pathmarks*, ed. William McNeill (Cambridge University Press, 1998), pp. 97–135.

The German word for "countering," "*Ent-gegnung,*" means both en-countering and opposing, and further articulates the de-cision of gods and humans out of the needfulness which opens inceptively the truth of be-ing. Gods and humans need each other in order to come into their own. Their relation occurs in "owning over to" (*Übereignung*) and "owning to" (*Zueignung*): "Enowning owns god over to man in that enowning owns man to god" (C19; B26). The owning over of gods to humans occurs in the compelling needfulness of the gods, and humans are owned to gods in that they respond to the need of the gods and find their own (being) in response to the gods' need.

Heidegger notes that "owning to" and "owning over to" stand in an utmost "counter" since they bridge the abyss out of which enowning oc-curs. This abyss opens in the need of be-ing out of the self-refusal of be-ing. The relation between humans and gods is mediated in the cleft of be-ing by the "not" of be-ing: In be-ing's self-refusal (the "not" of be-ing) dwells the need of the gods which necessitates humans to become grounders of the abysmal opening of be-ing so that be-ing may occur as enowning.

One could link the three first aspects of enowning that Heidegger ar-ticulates in section 267 by saying that, out of a distress which arises in the occurring of the truth of be-ing as self-refusal, the en-ownment of being-t/here occurs in the (en)countering de-cision of humans and gods. This entails a differencing between be-ing and beings which marks the next as-pect of enowning.

> 4. Countering is the origin of the strife, which holds sway by setting be-ings* [*das Seiende*][4] free from their lostness in mere beingness. *Setting-free* [*ent-setzen*] distinguishes en-owning in its relation to beings* as such. En-ownment of being-t/here* lets being-t/here* become abiding* in what is non-ordinary vis-à-vis every kind of being. (C331; B470)

The countering of gods and humans is the origin of the *setting-free* of beings. In section 269, Heidegger meditates further on this "setting free." He calls it "a tuning" and "the originary rift of what has the character of

---

4. It does not seem appropriate to translate "*das Seiende*" as "a being." What is set free is not merely a being but beings as a whole.

tuning itself" (*der ursprüngliche Aufriss des Stimmungshaften selbst*) (C340; B483). Thus, "setting-free" occurs in a fundamental attunement which opens an originary site of be-ing. In colloquial German, "*ent-setzen*" means to be horrified or frightened. But if we take the word literally, it carries the primary meaning of being "set out," or, if we take into account the disclosive meaning of "*ent-*," of being "set-free." Beings are set free from their lostness in mere beingness into the non-ordinariness (*Ungewöhnlichkeit*) of their being. This occurrence is the same one that the "Echo" joining describes: in startled dismay, thinking experiences both beings' lostness in the dominance of machination and lived experience (their lostness into mere beingness) and the withdrawal of be-ing out of which beings are experienced in their strangeness. Set free from the lostness in machination, humans experience the "non-ordinariness" of be-ing in relation to beings.[5]

The setting free into this originary relation to beings in their strangeness *originates*, says Heidegger, in the countering encounter of gods and humans, which is enowned out of a distress (needfulness) which arises in be-ing's self-refusal. This suggests that we understand the first three moments of en-owning as somehow more originary than the setting-free of beings. However, this setting-free belongs to the occurrence of be-ing as en-owning. What originates in the countering encounter of gods and humans, the setting-free into an originary relation to beings, remains *within* this originating event. This means that there remains a difference between be-ing and beings, a difference we should not understand like the difference between two entities but rather as an occurrence, as a differencing which occurs within the essential swaying of be-ing. The next aspect of enowning articulates this differencing from the side of be-ing insofar as be-ing differentiates itself from beings in withdrawing from them.

5. But setting free, grasped out of the clearing of the t/here [*Da*], is simultaneously *the withdrawal* of enowning, namely that it withdraws from any re-presenting-calculation and holds sway as refusal. (C331; B470)

5. "*Ungewöhnlichkeit*" means "non-ordinariness," as Emad and Maly translate it, but it also carries the sense of strangeness, in this case the strangeness echoed in the experience of the withdrawal of being from beings.

Setting beings free from their lostness in machination to the strangeness of be-ing occurs *as* the *withdrawal* of enowning from calculability.
At this point, it is important to note that the occurrence of be-ing as
withdrawal does not exhaust itself in its relation to the calculability of
beings. We may thus distinguish two intertwined senses of withdrawal:
the more originary sense refers to the withdrawal which echoes in the
distress of the gods; it is also the originary refusal out of which enowning
occurs. The withdrawal of be-ing (as enowning withdrawal) from calculability, i.e., from representational thought, is rooted in the primordial
withdrawal. If we understand the withdrawal of be-ing only in reference
to the fact that it cannot be re-presented, if we think that the withdrawal
is nothing but the other side of the represented thing, we do not do justice to Heidegger's thought because we would still be thinking metaphysically, i.e., with primary reference to beings. The essential swaying
of be-ing, however, is not just the be-ing *of* beings. This may be why
Heidegger stresses again and again that there is no immediate relation
between be-ing as enowning withdrawal and beings, even if a being
shelters the truth of be-ing: "[. . .] a being continues to belong to be-ing
as the *preserving* of its truth, but a being can never transfer itself into the
essential swaying of be-ing" (C334; B474). Why not? Because the essential swaying of be-ing occurs in (but not only in) the "not" of beings,
because the withdrawal of be-ing is precisely what withdraws in the
concealing-sheltering [*ver*bergen] of truth.

In section 268, Heidegger further clarifies the relation between enowning and beings (that "take place" in enowning):

> Be-ing holds sway as the en-ownment of gods and humans* to their
> countering. The strife of world and earth arises in the clearing of the
> sheltering of the "between" [*Zwischen*], which comes forth from within
> and along with the countering enownment. And only in the free-play of
> time-space of this strife is there preserving and loss of enownment and
> does that which is called a being enter the open of that clearing. (C336;
> B477)

The setting-free of beings in the withdrawal of enowning occurs
through the mediation of the strife of earth and world, i.e., in the disclosure of a world in relation to the self-secluding of an earth which is dis-

closed and also concealed in beings (be they natural things, utensils, works of art, words). This also means that be-ing as enowning does not echo as much in things "themselves" as in the earth and world that they shelter and conceal.

While the first five moments of en-owning focus on different aspects of the differencing, i.e., the de-cision in which en-owning occurs, the last three moments of enowning focus mainly on its gathering aspect. These en-ownings are called "simpleness," "uniqueness," and "aloneness." The most common misunderstanding to which these names give rise is to associate them with things. But the reader should keep in mind that these designations of en-owning do not abolish the primordial differencing in which enowning occurs and, with it, the "not" which permeates be-ing at its source.

The *"simpleness"* of en-owning is determined by the in-between (*Zwischen*) that occurs without mediation "as the ground of the countering ones in it" (C331; B471). This "in-between" is being-t/here conceived as the point of turning of enowning where gods and humans are both de-cided by an unbridgeable fissure, and yet are owned to each other; where be-ing sways as being set out and withdrawing from beings, and yet is sheltered in this withdrawal through beings.

The *"uniqueness"* of be-ing as enowning points to the fact that it does not need to—indeed cannot—be understood in relation to or as different from anything, "not even the difference from beings"[6] (C331f; B471). Any discourse about something "outside" of be-ing as enowning does not make sense if we think out of being-t/here. Thought from within being-t/here, be-ing cannot be understood as the ultimate "container" of everything, which would suggest some "outside" of the container. Be-ing occurs historically, finitely, and determinately in manifold ways of enowning, concealing, sheltering, forgetting, creating, preserving. Its uniqueness never abolishes the manifold modes of concrete historical being; instead, it designates this concreteness, historicality, and finitude in each mode of being.

6. This is how Heidegger approaches the question of being in the horizon of *Being and Time*.

"*Aloneness*" is rooted in be-ing's uniqueness and is perhaps the strangest designation of en-owning. Since there is nothing from which be-ing is set apart or in relation to which be-ing is understood, be-ing "surrounds itself only with the nothing" (C332; B471), a "nothing" which echoes possibly in the stillness which we find at the core of be-ing's occurrence as enowning withdrawal as a silence beyond words.

AFTERWORD

Contributions to Philosophy (From Enowning) is the first in a sequence of books[1] that contain what may be called Heidegger's esoteric writings. They are esoteric *not* in the sense that they contain some secret religious or mystical teachings. Rather, they are esoteric in the sense of the Greek word *"esoterikos,"* i.e., they are intimate, thought more from within, in the sense that they are not written in regards to the dominant public discourse. *Contributions* contains Heidegger's most intimate struggle to think at the edge of words and to bring to language what remains beyond written or spoken words, i.e., the struggle of the giving of these words themselves, the attuned-attuning silence out of which original thinking and saying arise.

At its best, an introduction to Heidegger's *Contributions to Philosophy* should "lead into" (intro-duce) this most intimate struggle of Heidegger's thinking. Whether it succeeds in this endeavor is not solely up to its author. If it succeeds in this endeavor, the reader will find an opening, not only to some understanding of the concealed realm out of which all of Heidegger's public writings since the thirties have arisen, but also to the other "esoteric" writings that follow *Contributions,* of which currently only *Besinnung* and *Die Geschichte des Seyns* have been published (and only in German). Of these writings, *Contributions* appears to be the work which is still most systematic in its structure because of its articulation into six joinings. The reader may be tempted to believe that in understanding this structure she understands the core of Heidegger's philosophy. However, what Heidegger says at the beginning of *Die Geschichte des Seyns* may call her back to a more modest stance: "'*Contributions*' are still frame but not a jointure, '*Besinnung*' is a center but not source" (GA 69, p. 5). Whether any of Heidegger's "esoteric" writings reach the source remains an open and certainly a disputable question.

---

1. Most of these works are not yet published; among these are *Über den Anfang* (GA 70), *Das Ereignis* (GA 71), *Die Stege des Anfangs* (GA 72), and *Gedachtes* (GA 81).

Index

DANIELA VALLEGA-NEU is Assistant Professor of Philosophy at California State University, Stanislaus. She is the author of *Die Notwendigkeit der Gründung im Zeitalter der Dekonstruktion* and coeditor of *Companion to Heidegger's* Contributions to Philosophy (Indiana University Press).